Robert Browning

Dramatis Personae

Robert Browning

Dramatis Personae

ISBN/EAN: 9783337304324

Printed in Europe, USA, Canada, Australia, Japan

Cover: Foto ©Thomas Meinert / pixelio.de

More available books at **www.hansebooks.com**

DRAMATIS PERSONÆ.

BY

ROBERT BROWNING.

SECOND EDITION.

LONDON:
CHAPMAN AND HALL, 193 PICCADILLY.
1864.

CONTENTS.

	PAGE
JAMES LEE	3
GOLD HAIR: A LEGEND OF PORNIC	27
THE WORST OF IT	37
DIS ALITER VISUM; OR, LE BYRON DE NOS JOURS	47
TOO LATE	57
ABT VOGLER	67
RABBI BEN EZRA	77
A DEATH IN THE DESERT	91
CALIBAN UPON SETEBOS; OR, NATURAL THEOLOGY IN THE ISLAND	123
CONFESSIONS	139
MAY AND DEATH	145
PROSPICE	147

CONTENTS.

	PAGE
YOUTH AND ART	153
A FACE	161
A LIKENESS	165
MR. SLUDGE, "THE MEDIUM"	171
APPARENT FAILURE	239
EPILOGUE	245

JAMES LEE.

JAMES LEE.

I.

JAMES LEE'S WIFE SPEAKS AT THE WINDOW.

1.

AH, love, but a day,
   And the world has changed!
The sun 's away,
   And the bird 's estranged;
The wind has dropped,
   And the sky 's deranged:
Summer has stopped.

2.

Look in my eyes!
   Wilt thou change too?
Should I fear surprise?
   Shall I find aught new
In the old and dear,
   In the good and true,
With the changing year?

3.

Thou art a man,
   But I am thy love!
For the lake, its swan;
   For the dell, its dove;
And for thee—(oh, haste!)
   Me, to bend above,
Me, to hold embraced!

II.

BY THE FIRESIDE.

1.

Is all our fire of shipwreck wood,
   Oak and pine?
Oh, for the ills half-understood,
   The dim, dead woe
   Long ago
Befallen this bitter coast of France!
Well, poor sailors took their chance;
   I take mine.

2.

A ruddy shaft our fire must shoot
   O'er the sea:
Do sailors eye the casement—mute,
   Drenched and stark,
   From their bark—
And envy, gnash their teeth for hate
O' the warm safe house and happy freight
   — Thee and me?

3.

God help you, sailors, at your need!
   Spare the curse!
For some ships, safe in port indeed,
   Rot and rust,
   Run to dust,
All through worms i' the wood, which crept,
Gnawed our hearts out while we slept:
   That is worse!

4.

Who lived here before us two?
   Old-world pairs!
Did a woman ever—would I knew!—
   Watch the man
   With whom began
Love's voyage full-sail,—(now, gnash your teeth!)
When planks start, open hell beneath
   Unawares?

III.

IN THE DOORWAY.

1.

The swallow has set her six young on the rail,
  And looks sea-ward:
The water's in stripes like a snake, olive-pale
  To the leeward,—
On the weather-side, black, spotted white with the
    wind:
" Good fortune departs, and disaster's behind,"—
Hark, the wind with its wants and its infinite wail!

2.

Our fig-tree, that leaned for the saltness, has furled
  Her five fingers,
Each leaf like a hand opened wide to the world
  Where there lingers
No glint of the gold, Summer sent for her sake:
How the vines writhe in rows, each impaled on its
    stake!
My heart shrivels up, and my spirit shrinks curled.

3.

Yet here are we two; we have love, house enough,
    With the field there,
This house of four rooms, that field red and rough,
    Though it yield there,
For the rabbit that robs, scarce a blade or a bent;
If a magpie alight now, it seems an event;
And they both will be gone at November's rebuff.

4.

But why must cold spread? but wherefore bring change
    To the spirit,
God meant should mate His with an infinite range,
    And inherit
His power to put life in the darkness and cold?
Oh, live and love worthily, bear and be bold!
Whom Summer made friends of, let Winter estrange!

JAMES LEE.

IV.

ALONG THE BEACH.

1.

I will be quiet and talk with you,
   And reason why you are wrong:
You wanted my love—is that much true?
And so I did love, so I do:
   What has come of it all along?

2.

I took you—how could I otherwise?
   For a world to me, and more;
For all, love greatens and glorifies
Till God 's a-glow, to the loving eyes,
   In what was mere earth before.

3.

Yes, earth—yes, mere ignoble earth!
   Now do I mis-state, mistake?
Do I wrong your weakness and call it worth?
Expect all harvest, dread no dearth,
   Seal my sense up for your sake?

4.

Oh, love, love, no, love! not so, indeed!
   You were just weak earth, I knew:
With much in you waste, with many a weed,
And plenty of passions run to seed,
   But a little good grain too.

5.

And such as you were, I took you for mine:
   Did not you find me yours,
To watch the olive and wait the vine,
And wonder when rivers of oil and wine
   Would flow, as the Book assures?

6.

Well, and if none of these good things came,
   What did the failure prove?
The man was my whole world, all the same,
With his flowers to praise, or his weeds to blame,
   And, either or both, to love.

7.

Yet this turns now to a fault—there! there!
   That I do love, watch too long,
And wait too well, and weary and wear;
And 'tis all an old story, and my despair
   Fit subject for some new song:

8.

How the light, light love, he has wings to fly
   At suspicion of a bond:
How my wisdom has bidden your pleasure good-bye,
Which will turn up next in a laughing eye,
   And why should you look beyond?

V.

ON THE CLIFF.

1.

I leaned on the turf,
I looked at a rock
Left dry by the surf;
For the turf, to call it grass were to mock:
Dead to the roots, so deep was done
The work of the summer sun.

2.

And the rock lay flat
As an anvil's face:
No iron like that!
Baked dry; of a weed, of a shell, no trace:
Sunshine outside, but ice at the core,
Death's altar by the lone shore.

3.

On the turf, sprang gay
With his films of blue,
No cricket, I'll say,
But a warhorse, barded and chanfroned too,
The gift of a quixote-mage to his knight,
Real fairy, with wings all right.

4.

On the rock, they scorch
Like a drop of fire
From a brandished torch,
Fell two red fans of a butterfly:
No turf, no rock, in their ugly stead,
See, wonderful blue and red!

5.

Is it not so
With the minds of men?
The level and low,
The burnt and bare, in themselves; but then
With such a blue and red grace, not theirs,
Love settling unawares!

VI.

READING A BOOK, UNDER THE CLIFF.

1.

"Still ailing, Wind? Wilt be appeased or no?
   Which needs the other's office, thou or I?
Dost want to be disburthened of a woe,
   And can, in truth, my voice untie
Its links, and let it go?

2.

"Art thou a dumb, wronged thing that would be righted,
   Entrusting thus thy cause to me? Forbear.
No tongue can mend such pleadings; faith, requited
   With falsehood,—love, at last aware
Of scorn,—hopes, early blighted,—

3.

"We have them; but I know not any tone
   So fit as thine to falter forth a sorrow:
Dost think men would go mad without a moan,
   If they knew any way to borrow
A pathos like thy own?

4.

"Which sigh wouldst mock, of all the sighs? The one
   So long escaping from lips starved and blue,
That lasts while on her pallet-bed the nun
   Stretches her length; her foot comes through
The straw she shivers on;

5.

"You had not thought she was so tall: and spent,
   Her shrunk lids open, her lean fingers shut
Close, close, their sharp and livid nails indent
   The clammy palm; then all is mute:
That way, the spirit went.

6.

"Or wouldst thou rather that I understand
   Thy will to help me?—like the dog I found
Once, pacing sad this solitary strand,
   Who would not take my food, poor hound,
But whined and licked my hand."

7.

All this, and more, comes from some young man's pride
   Of power to see,—in failure and mistake,
Relinquishment, disgrace, on every side,—
   Merely examples for his sake,
Helps to his path untried:

8.

Instances he must—simply recognize?
  Oh, more than so!—must, with a learner's zeal,
Make doubly prominent, twice emphasize,
  By added touches that reveal
The god in babe's disguise.

9.

Oh, he knows what defeat means, and the rest!
  Himself the undefeated that shall be:
Failure, disgrace, he flings them you to test,—
  His triumph, in eternity
Too plainly manifest!

10.

Whence, judge if he learn forthwith what the wind
  Means in its moaning—by the happy, prompt,
Instinctive way of youth, I mean; for kind
  Calm years, exacting their accompt
Of pain, mature the mind:

11.

And some midsummer morning, at the lull
  Just about daybreak, as he looks across
A sparkling foreign country, wonderful
  To the sea's edge for gloom and gloss,
Next minute must annul,—

12.

Then, when the wind begins among the vines,
    So low, so low, what shall it mean but this?
" Here is the change beginning, here the lines
    Circumscribe beauty, set to bliss
The limit time assigns."

13.

Nothing can be as it has been before;
    Better, so call it, only not the same.
To draw one beauty into our hearts' core,
    And keep it changeless! such our claim;
So answered,—Never more!

14.

Simple? Why this is the old woe o' the world;
    Tune, to whose rise and fall we live and die.
Rise with it, then! Rejoice that man is hurled
    From change to change unceasingly.
His soul's wings never furled!

15.

That's a new question; still replies the fact,
    Nothing endures: the wind moans, saying so;
We moan in acquiescence: there's life's pact,
    Perhaps probation—do *I* know?
God does: endure His act!

16.

Only, for man, how bitter not to grave
   On his soul's hands' palms one fair, good, wise thing
Just as he grasped it! For himself, death's wave;
   While time first washes—ah, the sting!—
O'er all he'd sink to save.

VII.

AMONG THE ROCKS.

1.

Oh, good gigantic smile o' the brown old earth,
   This autumn morning! How he sets his bones
To bask i' the sun, and thrusts out knees and feet
For the ripple to run over in its mirth;
   Listening the while, where on the heap of stones
The white breast of the sea-lark twitters sweet.

2.

That is the doctrine, simple, ancient, true;
   Such is life's trial, as old earth smiles and knows.
If you loved only what were worth your love,
Love were clear gain, and wholly well for you:
   Make the low nature better by your throes!
Give earth yourself, go up for gain above!

VIII.

BESIDE THE DRAWING-BOARD.

1.

"As like as a Hand to another Hand:"
　Whoever said that foolish thing,
Could not have studied to understand
　The counsels of God in fashioning,
Out of the infinite love of His heart,
This Hand, whose beauty I praise, apart
From the world of wonder left to praise,
If I tried to learn the other ways
Of love, in its skill, or love, in its power.
"As like as a Hand to another Hand:"
Who said that, never took his stand,
Found and followed, like me, an hour,
The beauty in this,—how free, how fine
To fear, almost,—of the limit-line!
As I looked at this, and learned and drew,
Drew and learned, and looked again,
While fast the happy minutes flew,
Its beauty mounted into my brain,
And a fancy seized me; I was fain

To efface my work, begin anew,
Kiss what before I only drew;
Ay, laying the red chalk 'twixt my lips,
With soul to help if the mere lips failed,
I kissed all right where the drawing ailed,
Kissed fast the grace that somehow slips
Still from one's soulless finger-tips.

2.

Go, little girl, with the poor coarse hand!
I have my lesson, shall understand.

IX.

ON DECK.

1.

There is nothing to remember in me,
   Nothing I ever said with a grace,
Nothing I did that you cared to see,
   Nothing I was that deserves a place
In your mind, now I leave you, set you free.

2.

Conceded! In turn, concede to me,
   Such things have been as a mutual flame.
Your soul's locked fast; but, love for a key,
   You might let it loose, till I grew the same
In your eyes, as in mine you stand : strange plea!

3.

For then, then, what would it matter to me
   That I was the harsh, ill-favoured one?
We both should be like as pea and pea;
   It was ever so since the world begun :
So, let me proceed with my reverie.

4.

How strange it were if you had all me,
    As I have all you in my heart and brain,
You, whose least word brought gloom or glee,
    Who never lifted the hand in vain
Will hold mine yet, from over the sea!

5.

Strange, if a face, when you thought of me,
    Rose like your own face present now,
With eyes as dear in their due degree,
    Much such a mouth, and as bright a brow,
Till you saw yourself, while you cried " 'Tis She!"

6.

Well, you may, or you must, set down to me
    Love that was life, life that was love;
A tenure of breath at your lips' decree,
    A passion to stand as your thoughts approve,
A rapture to fall where your foot might be.

7.

But did one touch of such love for me
    Come in a word or a look of yours,
Whose words and looks will, circling, flee
    Round me and round while life endures,—
Could I fancy "As I feel, thus feels He;"

8.

Why, fade you might to a thing like me,
    And your hair grow these coarse hanks of hair,
And your skin, this bark of a gnarled tree,—
    You might turn myself; should I know or care,
When I should be dead of joy, James Lee?

GOLD HAIR:

A STORY OF PORNIC.

GOLD HAIR:

A STORY OF PORNIC.

1.

Oh, the beautiful girl, too white,
   Who lived at Pornic, down by the sea,
Just where the sea and the Loire unite!
   And a boasted name in Brittany
She bore, which I will not write.

2.

Too white, for the flower of life is red;
   Her flesh was the soft, seraphic screen
Of a soul that is meant (her parents said)
   To just see earth, and hardly be seen,
And blossom in Heaven instead.

3.

Yet earth saw one thing, one how fair!
   One grace that grew to its full on earth:
Smiles might be sparse on her cheek so spare,
   And her waist want half a girdle's girth,
But she had her great gold hair.

4.

Hair, such a wonder of flix and floss,
   Freshness and fragrance—floods of it, too!
Gold, did I say? Nay, gold's mere dross:
   Here, Life smiled, "Think what I meant to do!"
And Love sighed, "Fancy my loss!"

5.

So, when she died, it was scarce more strange
   Than that, when some delicate evening dies,
And you follow its spent sun's pallid range,
   There's a shoot of colour startles the skies
With sudden, violent change,—

6.

That, while the breath was nearly to seek,
   As they put the little cross to her lips,
She changed; a spot came out on her cheek,
   A spark from her eye in mid-eclipse,
And she broke forth, "I must speak!"

7.

"Not my hair!" made the girl her moan—
   "All the rest is gone or to go;
But the last, last grace, my all, my own,
   Let it stay in the grave, that the ghosts may know!
Leave my poor gold hair alone!"

8.

The passion thus vented, dead lay she;
   Her parents sobbed their worst on that,
All friends joined in, nor observed degree:
   For indeed the hair was to wonder at,
As it spread—not flowing free,

9.

But curled around her brow, like a crown,
   And coiled beside her cheeks, like a cap,
And calmed about her neck—ay, down
   To her breast, pressed flat, without a gap
I' the gold, it reached her gown.

10.

All kissed that face, like a silver wedge
   Mid the yellow wealth, nor disturbed its hair;
E'en the priest allowed death's privilege,
   As he planted the crucifix with care
On her breast, 'twixt edge and edge.

11.

And thus was she buried, inviolate
  Of body and soul, in the very space
By the altar; keeping saintly state
  In Pornic church, for her pride of race,
Pure life, and piteous fate.

12.

And in after-time would your fresh tear fall,
  Though your mouth might twitch with a dubious smile,
As they told you of gold both robe and pall,
  How she prayed them leave it alone awhile,
So it never was touched at all.

13.

Years flew; this legend grew at last
  The life of the lady; all she had done,
All been, in the memories fading fast
  Of lover and friend, was summed in one
Sentence survivors passed:

14.

To wit, she was meant for Heaven, not earth;
  Had turned an angel before the time:
Yet, since she was mortal, in such dearth
  Of frailty, all you could count a crime
Was—she knew her gold hair's worth.

15.

At little pleasant Pornic church,
    It chanced, the pavement wanted repair,
Was taken to pieces: left in the lurch,
    A certain sacred space lay bare,
And the boys began research.

16.

'Twas the space where our sires would lay a saint,
    A benefactor,—a bishop, suppose,
A baron with armour-adornments quaint,
    A dame with chased ring and jewelled rose,
Things sanctity saves from taint;

17.

So we come to find them in after-days
    When the corpse is presumed to have done with gauds
Of use to the living, in many ways:
    For the boys get pelf, and the town applauds,
And the church deserves the praise.

18.

They grubbed with a will: and at length—*O cor*
    Humanum, pectora cæca, and the rest!—
They found—no gauds they were prying for,
    No ring, no rose, but—who would have guessed?—
A double Louis-d'or!

19.

Here was a case for the priest: he heard,
   Marked, inwardly digested, laid
Finger on nose, smiled, "A little bird
   Chirps in my ear:" then, "Bring a spade,
Dig deeper!"—he gave the word.

20.

And lo, when they came to the coffin-lid,
   Or the rotten planks which composed it once,
Why, there lay the girl's skull wedged amid
   A mint of money, it served for the nonce
To hold in its hair-heaps hid!

21.

Hid there? Why? Could the girl be wont
   (She, the stainless soul) to treasure up
Money, earth's trash and Heaven's affront?
   Had a spider found out the communion-cup,
Was a toad in the christening-font?

22.

Truth is truth: too true it was.
   Gold! She hoarded and hugged it first,
Longed for it, leaned o'er it, loved it—alas—
   Till the humour grew to a head and burst,
And she cried, at the final pass,—

23.

"Talk not of God, my heart is stone!
  Nor lover nor friend—be gold for both!
Gold I lack; and, my all, my own,
  It shall hide in my hair.   I scarce die loth,
If they let my hair alone!"

24.

Louis-d'ors, some six times five,
  And duly double, every piece.
Now, do you see?   With the priest to shrive,
  With parents preventing her soul's release
By kisses that kept alive,—

25.

With Heaven's gold gates about to ope,
  With friends' praise, gold-like, lingering still,
An instinct had bidden the girl's hand grope
  For gold, the true sort—"Gold in Heaven, if you will;
But I keep earth's too, I hope."

26.

Enough!   The priest took the grave's grim yield:
  The parents, they eyed that price of sin
As if *thirty pieces* lay revealed
  On the place *to bury strangers in,*
The hideous Potter's Field.

27.

But the priest bethought him: "'Milk that's spilt'
—You know the adage! Watch and pray!
Saints tumble to earth with so slight a tilt!

It would build a new altar; that, we may!"
And the altar therewith was built.

28.

Why I deliver this horrible verse?

As the text of a sermon, which now I preach:
Evil or good may be better or worse

In the human heart, but the mixture of each
Is a marvel and a curse.

29.

The candid incline to surmise of late

That the Christian faith may be false, I find;
For our Essays-and-Reviews' debate

Begins to tell on the public mind,
And Colenso's words have weight:

30.

I still, to suppose it true, for my part,

See reasons and reasons; this, to begin:
'Tis the faith that launched point-blank her dart

At the head of a lie—taught Original Sin,
The Corruption of Man's Heart.

THE WORST OF IT.

THE WORST OF IT.

1.

Would it were I had been false, not you!
  I that am nothing, not you that are all:
I, never the worse for a touch or two
  On my speckled hide; not you, the pride
Of the day, my swan, that a first fleck's fall
  On her wonder of white must unswan, undo!

2.

I had dipped in life's struggle, and out again,
  Bore specks of it here, there, easy to see,
When I found my swan and the cure was plain;
  The dull turned bright as I caught your white
On my bosom: you saved me—saved in vain
  If you ruined yourself, and all through me!

3.

Yes, all through the speckled beast that I am,
    Who taught you to stoop; you gave me yourself,
And bound your soul by the vows that damn:
    Since on better thought you break, as you ought,
Vows—words, no angel set down, some elf
    Mistook,—for an oath, an epigram!

4.

Yes, might I judge you, here were my heart,
    And a hundred its like, to treat as you pleased!
I choose to be yours, for my proper part,
    Yours, leave or take, or mar me or make;
If I acquiesce, why should you be teased
    With the conscience-prick and the memory-smart?

5.

But what will God say? Oh, my sweet,
    Think, and be sorry you did this thing!
Though earth were unworthy to feel your feet,
    There's a Heaven above may deserve your love:
Should you forfeit Heaven for a snapt gold ring
    And a promise broke, were it just or meet?

6.

And I to have tempted you! I, who tried
   Your soul, no doubt, till it sank! Unwise,
I loved, and was lowly, loved and aspired,
   Loved, grieving or glad, till I made you mad,
And you meant to have hated and despised—
   Whereas, you deceived me nor inquired!

7.

She, ruined? How? No Heaven for her?
   Crowns to give, and none for the brow
That looked like marble and smelt like myrrh?
   Shall the robe be worn, and the palm-branch borne,
And she go graceless, she graced now
   Beyond all saints, as themselves aver?

8.

Hardly! That must be understood!
   The earth is your place of penance, then;
And what will it prove? I desire your good,
   But, plot as I may, I can find no way
How a blow should fall, such as falls on men,
   Nor prove too much for your womanhood.

9.

It will come, I suspect, at the end of life,
    When you walk alone, and review the past;
And I, who so long shall have done with strife,
    And journeyed my stage, and earned my wage,
And retired as was right,—I am called at last
    When the devil stabs you, to lend the knife.

10.

He stabs for the minute of trivial wrong,
    Nor the other hours are able to save,
The happy, that lasted my whole life long:
    For a promise broke, not for first words spoke,
The true, the only, that turn my grave
    To a blaze of joy and a crash of song.

11.

Witness beforehand! Off I trip
    On a safe path gay through the flowers you flung:
My very name made great by your lip,
    And my heart a-glow with the good I know
Of a perfect year when we both were young,
    And I tasted the angels' fellowship.

12.

And witness, moreover . . . Ah, but wait!
  I spy the loop whence an arrow shoots!
It may be for yourself, when you meditate,
  That you grieve—for slain ruth, murdered truth:
"Though falsehood escape in the end, what boots?
  How truth would have triumphed!"—you sigh too
    late.

13.

Ay, who would have triumphed like you, I say!
  Well, it is lost now; well, you must bear,
Abide and grow fit for a better day:
  You should hardly grudge, could I be your judge!
But hush! For you, can be no despair:
  There 's amends: 'tis a secret: hope and pray!

14.

For I was true at least—oh, true enough!
  And, dear, truth is not as good as it seems!
Commend me to conscience! Idle stuff!
  Much help is in mine, as I mope and pine,
And skulk through day, and scowl in my dreams
  At my swan's obtaining the crow's rebuff.

15.

Men tell me of truth now—"False!" I cry:
   Of beauty—"A mask, friend! Look beneath!
We take our own method, the devil and I,
   With pleasant and fair and wise and rare:
And the best we wish to what lives, is—death;
   Which even in wishing, perhaps we lie!

16.

Far better commit a fault and have done—
   As you, dear!—for ever; and choose the pure,
And look where the healing waters run,
   And strive and strain to be good again,
And a place in the other world insure,
   All glass and gold, with God for its sun.

17.

Misery! What shall I say or do?
   I cannot advise, or, at least, persuade:
Most like, you are glad you deceived me—rue
   No whit of the wrong: you endured too long,
Have done no evil and want no aid,
   Will live the old life out and chance the new.

18.

And your sentence is written all the same,
    And I can do nothing,—pray, perhaps:
But somehow the world pursues its game,
    If I pray, if I curse,—for better or worse:
And my faith is torn to a thousand scraps,
    And my heart feels ice while my words breathe flame.

19.

Dear, I look from my hiding-place.
    Are you still so fair? Have you still the eyes?
Be happy! Add but the other grace,
    Be good! Why want what the angels vaunt?
I knew you once: but in Paradise,
    If we meet, I will pass nor turn my face.

DÎS ALITER VISUM;

OR,

LE BYRON DE NOS JOURS.

DIS ALITER VISUM;

OR,

LE BYRON DE NOS JOURS.

———◆◦◆———

1.

Stop, let me have the truth of that!
   Is that all true? I say, the day
Ten years ago when both of us
   Met on a morning, friends—as thus
We meet this evening, friends or what?—

2.

Did you—because I took your arm
   And sillily smiled, "A mass of brass
That sea looks, blazing underneath!"
   While up the cliff-road edged with heath,
We took the turns nor came to harm—

3.

Did you consider " Now makes twice
   That I have seen her, walked and talked
With this poor pretty thoughtful thing,
   Whose worth I weigh: she tries to sing;
Draws, hopes in time the eye grows nice;

4.

" Reads verse and thinks she understands;
   Loves all, at any rate, that's great,
Good, beautiful; but much as we
   Down at the Bath-house love the sea,
Who breathe its salt and bruise its sands:

5.

" While . . do but follow the fishing-gull
   That flaps and floats from wave to cave!
There's the sea-lover, fair my friend!
   What then? Be patient, mark and mend!
Had you the making of your scull?"

6.

And did you, when we faced the church
   With spire and sad slate roof, aloof
From human fellowship so far,
   Where a few graveyard crosses are,
And garlands for the swallows' perch,—

7.

Did you determine, as we stepped
    O'er the lone stone fence, " Let me get
Her for myself, and what 's the earth
    With all its art, verse, music, worth—
Compared with love, found, gained, and kept?

8.

" Schumann 's our music-maker now;
    Has his march-movement youth and mouth?
Ingres 's the modern man that paints;
    Which will lean on me, of his saints?
Heine for songs; for kisses, how?"

9.

And did you, when we entered, reached
    The votive frigate, soft aloft
Riding on air this hundred years,
    Safe-smiling at old hopes and fears,—
Did you draw profit while she preached?

10.

Resolving " Fools we wise men grow!
    Yes, I could easily blurt out curt
Some question that might find reply
    As prompt in her stopped lips, dropped eye,
And rush of red to cheek and brow:

11.

" Thus were a match made, sure and fast,
   'Mid the blue weed-flowers round the mound
Where, issuing, we shall stand and stay
   For one more look at Baths and bay,
Sands, sea-gulls, and the old church last—

12.

" A match 'twixt me, bent, wigged, and lamed,
   Famous, however, for verse and worse,
Sure of the Fortieth spare Arm-chair
   When gout and glory seat me there,
So, one whose love-freaks pass unblamed,—

13.

" And this young beauty, round and sound
   As a mountain-apple, youth and truth
With loves and doves, at all events
   With money in the Three per Cents;
Whose choice of me would seem profound:—

14.

" She might take me as I take her.
   . Perfect the hour would pass, alas!
Climb high, love high, what matter? Still,
Feet, feelings, must descend the hill:
   An hour's perfection can't recur.

15.

" Then follows Paris and full time
   For both to reason: ' Thus with us!'
She'll sigh, ' Thus girls give body and soul
   At first word, think they gain the goal,
When 'tis the starting-place they climb!

16.

" ' My friend makes verse and gets renown;
   Have they all fifty years, his peers?
He knows the world, firm, quiet, and gay;
   Boys will become as much one day:
They're fools; he cheats, with beard less brown.

17.

" ' For boys say, *Love me or I die!*
   He did not say, *The truth is, youth*
I want, who am old and know too much;
   I'd catch youth: lend me sight and touch!
Drop heart's blood where life's wheels grate dry!

18.

" While I should make rejoinder "—(then
   It was, no doubt, you ceased that least
Light pressure of my arm in yours)
   " ' I can conceive of cheaper cures
For a yawning-fit o'er books and men.

19.

" ' What? All I am, was, and might be,
   All, books taught, art brought, life's whole strife,
Painful results since precious, just
   Were fitly exchanged in wise disgust
For two cheeks freshened by youth and sea?

20.

" ' All for a nosegay!—what came first;
   With fields on flower, untried each side;
I rally, need my books and men,
   And find a nosegay: drop it, then,
No match yet made for best or worst!' "

21.

That ended me. You judged the porch
   We left by, Norman; took our look
At sea and sky; wondered so few
   Find out the place for air and view;
Remarked the sun began to scorch;

22.

Descended, soon regained the Baths,
   And then, good bye! Years ten since then:
Ten years! We meet: you tell me, now,
   By a window-seat for that cliff-brow,
On carpet-stripes for those sand-paths.

23.

Now I may speak: you fool, for all
   Your lore! Who made things plain in vain?
What was the sea for? What, the grey
   Sad church, that solitary day,
Crosses and graves and swallows' call?

24.

Was there nought better than to enjoy?
   No feat which, done, would make time break,
And let us pent-up creatures through
   Into eternity, our due?
No forcing earth teach Heaven's employ?

25.

No wise beginning, here and now,
   What cannot grow complete (earth's feat)
And Heaven must finish, there and then?
   No tasting earth's true food for men,
Its sweet in sad, its sad in sweet?

26.

No grasping at love, gaining a share
   O' the sole spark from God's life at strife
With death, so, sure of range above
   The limits here? For us and love,
Failure; but, when God fails, despair.

27.

This you call wisdom? Thus you add
  Good unto good again, in vain?
You loved, with body worn and weak;
  I loved, with faculties to seek:
Were both loves worthless since ill-clad?

28.

Let the mere star-fish in his vault
  Crawl in a wash of weed, indeed,
Rose-jacynth to the finger-tips:
  He, whole in body and soul, outstrips
Man, found with either in default.

29.

But what's whole, can increase no more,
  Is dwarfed and dies, since here 's its sphere.
The devil laughed at you in his sleeve!
  You knew not? That, I well believe;
Or you had saved two souls: nay, four.

30.

For Stephanie sprained last night her wrist,
  Ancle, or something. "Pooh," cry you?
At any rate she danced, all say,
  Vilely: her vogue has had its day.
Here comes my husband from his whist.

TOO LATE.

TOO LATE.

1.

Here was I with my arm and heart
   And brain, all yours for a word, a want
Put into a look—just a look, your part,—
   While mine, to repay it . . . vainest vaunt,
Were the woman, that's dead, alive to hear,
   Had her lover, that's lost, love's proof to show!
But I cannot show it; you cannot speak
   From the churchyard neither, miles removed,
Though I feel by a pulse within my cheek,
   Which stabs and stops, that the woman I loved
Needs help in her grave and finds none near,
   Wants warmth from the heart which sends it—so!

2

Did I speak once angrily, all the drear days
   You lived, you woman I loved so well,
Who married the other? Blame or praise,
   Where was the use then? Time would tell,
And the end declare what man for you,
   What woman for me was the choice of God.
But, Edith dead! no doubting more!
   I used to sit and look at my life
As it rippled and ran till, right before,
   A great stone stopped it: oh, the strife
Of waves at that stone some devil threw
   In my life's midcurrent, thwarting God!

3.

But either I thought, " They may churn and chide
   Awhile, my waves which came for their joy
And found this horrible stone full-tide:
   Yet I see just a thread escape, deploy
Through the evening-country, silent and safe,
   And it suffers no more till it finds the sea."
Or else I would think, " Perhaps some night
   When new things happen, a meteor-ball
May slip through the sky in a line of light,
   And earth breathe hard, and landmarks fall,
And my waves no longer champ nor chafe,   [be!"
   Since a stone will have rolled from its place: let

4.

But, dead! All's done with: wait who may,
 Watch and wear and wonder who will.
Oh, my whole life that ends to-day!
 Oh, my soul's sentence, sounding still,
" The woman is dead, that was none of his;
 And the man, that was none of hers, may go!"
There's only the past left: worry that!
 Wreak, like a bull, on the empty coat,
Rage, its late wearer is laughing at!
 Tear the collar to rags, having missed his throat;
Strike stupidly on—" This, this and this,
 Where I would that a bosom received the blow!"

5.

I ought to have done more: once my speech,
 And once your answer, and there, the end,
And Edith was henceforth out of reach!
 Why, men do more to deserve a friend,
Be rid of a foe, get rich, grow wise,
 Nor, folding their arms, stare fate in the face.
Why, better even have burst like a thief
 And borne you away to a rock for us two
In a moment's horror, bright, bloody and brief,
 Then changed to myself again—" I slew
Myself in that moment; a ruffian lies
 Somewhere: your slave, see, born in his place!"

6.

What did the other do? You be judge!
   Look at us, Edith! Here are we both!
Give him his six whole years: I grudge
   None of the life with you, nay, I loathe
Myself that I grudged his start in advance
   Of me who could overtake and pass.
But, as if he loved you! No, not he,
   Nor anyone else in the world, 'tis plain:
Who ever heard that another, free
   As I, young, prosperous, sound and sane,
Poured life out, proffered it—" Half a glance
   Of those eyes of yours and I drop the glass!"

7.

Handsome, were you? 'Tis more than they held,
   More than they said; I was 'ware and watched:
I was the 'scapegrace, this rat belled
   The cat, this fool got his whiskers scratched:
The others? No head that was turned, no heart
   Broken, my lady, assure yourself!
Each soon made his mind up; so and so
   Married a dancer, such and such
Stole his friend's wife, stagnated slow,
   Or maundered, unable to do as much,
And muttered of peace where he had no part:
   While, hid in the closet, laid on the shelf,—

8.

On the whole, you were let alone, I think!
   So, you looked to the other, who acquiesced;
My rival, the proud man,—prize your pink
   Of poets! A poet he was! I've guessed:
He rhymed you his rubbish nobody read,
   Loved you and doved you—did not I laugh!
There was a prize! But we both were tried.
   Oh, heart of mine, marked broad with her mark,
Tekel, found wanting, set aside,
   Scorned! See, I bleed these tears in the dark
Till comfort come and the last be bled:
   He? He is tagging your epitaph.

9.

If it would only come over again!
   —Time to be patient with me, and probe
This heart till you punctured the proper vein,
   Just to learn what blood is: twitch the robe
From that blank lay-figure your fancy draped,
   Prick the leathern heart till the—verses spirt!
And late it was easy; late, you walked
   Where a friend might meet you; Edith's name
Arose to one's lip if one laughed or talked;
   If I heard good news, you heard the same;
When I woke, I knew that your breath escaped;
   I could bide my time, keep alive, alert.

10.

And alive I shall keep and long, you will see!
   I knew a man, was kicked like a dog
From gutter to cesspool; what cared he
   So long as he picked from the filth his prog?
He saw youth, beauty, and genius die,
   And jollily lived to his hundredth year.
But I will live otherwise: none of such life!
   At once I begin as I mean to end.
Go on with the world, get gold in its strife,
   Give your spouse the slip, and betray your friend!
There are two who decline, a woman and I,
   And enjoy our death in the darkness here.

11.

I liked that way you had with your curls
   Wound to a ball in a net behind:
Your cheek was chaste as a quaker-girl's,
   And your mouth—there was never, to my mind,
Such a funny mouth, for it would not shut;
   And the dented chin, too—what a chin!
There were certain ways when you spoke, some words
   That you know you never could pronounce:
You were thin, however; like a bird's
   Your hand seemed—some would say, the pounce
Of a scaly-footed hawk—all but!
   The world was right when it called you thin.

12.

But I turn my back on the world : I take
   Your hand, and kneel, and lay to my lips.
Bid me live, Edith ! Let me slake
   Thirst at your presence ! Fear no slips !
'Tis your slave shall pay, while his soul endures,
   Full due, love's whole debt, *summum jus.*
My queen shall have high observance, planned
   Courtship made perfect, no least line
Crossed without warrant. There you stand,
   Warm too, and white too : would this wine
Had washed all over that body of yours,
   Ere I drank it, and you down with it, thus !

ABT VOGLER.

(AFTER HE HAS BEEN EXTEMPORIZING UPON THE MUSICAL INSTRUMENT OF HIS INVENTION.)

The Abbot was a famous musician and organist, the teacher of Meyerbeer. Concerning the new kind of organ which he invented, and which he called an "Orchestricon" we know nothing save that its effects were merely amplifications of those belonging to an organ. The poem describes the awe and rapture which fill the soul of a great organist when the instrument shudders, soars, rejoices in his inspiration. It is not the description of a musical mood, but the showing of a man who has the mood. It is the exultation and religious feeling of a man in the very act. The noble lines are not fine things attempting to set forth the metaphysics of musical expression and enjoyment, but they represent a man at the very climax of his musical passion. Is the effect any the less dramatic because the man is not committing a murder, or conspiring, or seducing, or overreaching, or infecting an honest ear with jealousy? It is not so theatrical, because the emotion itself is not so broad and popular, but its inmost genius is dramatic.

Atlantic Monthly. 14:645.

ABT VOGLER.

1.

Would that the structure brave, the manifold music I build,
    Bidding my organ obey, calling its keys to their work,
Claiming each slave of the sound, at a touch, as when Solomon willed
    Armies of angels that soar, legions of demons that lurk,
Man, brute, reptile, fly,—alien of end and of aim,
    Adverse, each from the other heaven-high, hell-deep removed,—
Should rush into sight at once as he named the ineffable Name,
    And pile him a palace straight, to pleasure the princess he loved!

2.

Would it might tarry like his, the beautiful building of
  mine,
 This which my keys in a crowd pressed and impor-
  tuned to raise!
Ah, one and all, how they helped, would dispart now
  and now combine,
 Zealous to hasten the work, heighten their master
  his praise!
And one would bury his brow with a blind plunge down
  to hell,
 Burrow awhile and build, broad on the roots of
  things,
Then up again swim into sight, having based me my
  palace well,
 Founded it, fearless of flame, flat on the nether
  springs.

3.

And another would mount and march, like the excellent
  minion he was,
 Ay, another and yet another, one crowd but with
  many a crest,
Raising my rampired walls of gold as transparent as
  glass,
 Eager to do and die, yield each his place to the rest:

For higher still and higher (as a runner tips with fire,
    When a great illumination surprises a festal night—
Outlining round and round Rome's dome from space to spire)
    Up, the pinnacled glory reached, and the pride of my soul was in sight.

4.

In sight? Not half! for it seemed, it was certain, to match man's birth,
    Nature in turn conceived, obeying an impulse as I;
And the emulous heaven yearned down, made effort to reach the earth,
    As the earth had done her best, in my passion, to scale the sky:
Novel splendours burst forth, grew familiar and dwelt with mine,
    Not a point nor peak but found and fixed its wandering star;
Meteor-moons, balls of blaze: and they did not pale nor pine,
    For earth had attained to heaven, there was no more near nor far.

5.

Nay more; for there wanted not who walked in the
    glare and glow,
  Presences plain in the place; or, fresh from the Pro-
    toplast,
Furnished for ages to come, when a kindlier wind
    should blow,
  Lured now to begin and live, in a house to their
    liking at last;
Or else the wonderful Dead who have passed through
    the body and gone,
  But were back once more to breathe in an old world
    worth their new:
What never had been, was now; what was, as it shall
    be anon;
  And what is,—shall I say, matched both? for I was
    made perfect too.

6.

All through my keys that gave their sounds to a wish
    of my soul,
  All through my soul that praised as its wish flowed
    visibly forth,
All through music and me! For think, had I painted
    the whole,
  Why, there it had stood, to see, nor the process so
    wonder-worth:

Had I written the same, made verse—still, effect proceeds from cause,
   Ye know why the forms are fair, ye hear how the tale is told;
It is all triumphant art, but art in obedience to laws,
   Painter and poet are proud in the artist-list enrolled :—

7.

But here is the finger of God, a flash of the will that can,
   Existent behind all laws, that made them and, lo, they are!
And I know not if, save in this, such gift be allowed to man,
   That out of three sounds he frame, not a fourth sound, but a star.
Consider it well: each tone of our scale in itself is nought;
   It is everywhere in the world—loud, soft, and all is said:
Give it to me to use! I mix it with two in my thought;
   And, there! Ye have heard and seen: consider and bow the head!

8.

Well, it is gone at last, the palace of music I reared ;
   Gone ! and the good tears start, the praises that come
       too slow ;
For one is assured at first, one scarce can say that he
       feared,
   That he even gave it a thought, the gone thing was
       to go.
Never to be again ! But many more of the kind
   As good, nay, better perchance : is this your comfort
       to me ?
To me, who must be saved because I cling with my
       mind
   To the same, same self, same love, same God : ay,
       what was, shall be. *

9.

Therefore to whom turn I but to Thee, the ineffable
       Name ?
   Builder and maker, Thou, of houses not made with
       hands !
What, have fear of change from Thee who art ever the
       same ?
   Doubt that Thy power can fill the heart that Thy
       power expands ?

There shall never be one lost good! What was, shall
    live as before;
  The evil is null, is nought, is silence implying
    sound;
What was good, shall be good, with, for evil, so much
    good more;
  On the earth the broken arcs; in the heaven, a per-
    fect round.

10.

All we have willed or hoped or dreamed of good, shall
    exist;
  Not its semblance, but itself; no beauty, nor good,
    nor power
Whose voice has gone forth, but each survives for the
    melodist
  When eternity affirms the conception of an hour.
The high that proved too high, the heroic for earth too
    hard,
  The passion that left the ground to lose itself in the
    sky,
Are music sent up to God by the lover and the bard;
  Enough that He heard it once: we shall hear it by-
    and-by.

11.

And what is our failure here but a triumph's evidence
   For the fulness of the days? Have we withered or
      agonized?
Why else was the pause prolonged but that singing
      might issue thence?
   Why rushed the discords in, but that harmony should
      be prized?
Sorrow is hard to bear, and doubt is slow to clear,
   Each sufferer says his say, his scheme of the weal
      and woe:
But God has a few of us whom He whispers in the ear;
   The rest may reason and welcome: 'tis we musicians
      know.

12.

Well, it is earth with me; silence resumes her reign:
   I will be patient and proud, and soberly acquiesce.
Give me the keys. I feel for the common chord again,
   Sliding by semitones, till I sink to the minor,—yes,
And I blunt it into a ninth, and I stand on alien
      ground,
   Surveying a while the heights I rolled from into the
      deep;
Which, hark, I have dared and done, for my resting-
      place is found,
   The C Major of this life: so, now I will try to sleep.

RABBI BEN EZRA.

RABBI BEN EZRA.

1.

Grow old along with me!
The best is yet to be,
The last of life, for which the first was made:
Our times are in His hand
Who saith "A whole I planned,
Youth shows but half; trust God: see all, nor be afraid!"

2.

Not that, amassing flowers,
Youth sighed "Which rose make ours,
Which lily leave and then as best recall?"
Not that, admiring stars,
It yearned "Nor Jove, nor Mars;
Mine be some figured flame which blends, transcends them all!"

3.

Not for such hopes and fears
Annulling youth's brief years,
Do I remonstrate: folly wide the mark!
Rather I prize the doubt
Low kinds exist without,
Finished and finite clods, untroubled by a spark.

4.

Poor vaunt of life indeed,
Were man but formed to feed
On joy, to solely seek and find and feast:
Such feasting ended, then
As sure an end to men;
Irks care the crop-full bird? Frets doubt the maw-
    crammed beast?

5.

Rejoice we are allied
To That which doth provide
And not partake, effect and not receive!
A spark disturbs our clod;
Nearer we hold of God
Who gives, than of His tribes that take, I must believe.

6.

Then, welcome each rebuff
That turns earth's smoothness rough,
Each sting that bids nor sit nor stand but go!
Be our joys three-parts pain!
Strive, and hold cheap the strain;
Learn, nor account the pang; dare, never grudge the throe!

7.

For thence,—a paradox
Which comforts while it mocks,—
Shall life succeed in that it seems to fail:
What I aspired to be,
And was not, comforts me:
A brute I might have been, but would not sink i' the scale.

8.

What is he but a brute
Whose flesh hath soul to suit,
Whose spirit works lest arms and legs want play?
To man, propose this test—
Thy body at its best,
How far can that project thy soul on its lone way?

9.

Yet gifts should prove their use:
I own the Past profuse
Of power each side, perfection every turn:
Eyes, ears took in their dole,
Brain treasured up the whole;
Should not the heart beat once "How good to live and learn?"

10.

Not once beat "Praise be Thine!
I see the whole design,
I, who saw Power, see now Love perfect too:
Perfect I call Thy plan:
Thanks that I was a man!
Maker, remake, complete,—I trust what Thou shalt do!"

11.

For pleasant is this flesh;
Our soul, in its rose-mesh
Pulled ever to the earth, still yearns for rest:
Would we some prize might hold
To match those manifold
Possessions of the brute,—gain most, as we did best!

12.

Let us not always say
" Spite of this flesh to-day
I strove, made head, gained ground upon the whole!"
As the bird wings and sings,
Let us cry " All good things
Are ours, nor soul helps flesh more, now, than flesh
    helps soul!"

13.

Therefore I summon age
To grant youth's heritage,
Life's struggle having so far reached its term:
Thence shall I pass, approved
A man, for aye removed
From the developed brute; a God though in the germ.

14.

And I shall thereupon
Take rest, ere I be gone
Once more on my adventure brave and new:
Fearless and unperplexed,
When I wage battle next,
What weapons to select, what armour to indue.

15.

Youth ended, I shall try
My gain or loss thereby;
Be the fire ashes, what survives is gold:
And I shall weigh the same,
Give life its praise or blame:
Young, all lay in dispute; I shall know, being old.

16.

For note, when evening shuts,
A certain moment cuts
The deed off, calls the glory from the grey:
A whisper from the west
Shoots—" Add this to the rest,
Take it and try its worth: here dies another day."

17.

So, still within this life,
Though lifted o'er its strife,
Let me discern, compare, pronounce at last,
" This rage was right i' the main,
That acquiescence vain:
The Future I may face now I have proved the Past."

18.

For more is not reserved
To man, with soul just nerved
To act to-morrow what he learns to-day:
Here, work enough to watch
The Master work, and catch
Hints of the proper craft, tricks of the tool's true play.

19.

As it was better, youth
Should strive, through acts uncouth,
Toward making, than repose on aught found made;
So, better, age, exempt
From strife, should know, than tempt
Further. Thou waitedst age; wait death nor be afraid!

20.

Enough now, if the Right
And Good and Infinite
Be named here, as thou callest thy hand thine own,
With knowledge absolute,
Subject to no dispute
From fools that crowded youth, nor let thee feel alone.

21.

Be there, for once and all,
Severed great minds from small,
Announced to each his station in the Past!
Was I, the world arraigned,
Were they, my soul disdained,
Right? Let age speak the truth and give us peace at last!

22.

Now, who shall arbitrate?
Ten men love what I hate,
Shun what I follow, slight what I receive;
Ten, who in ears and eyes
Match me: we all surmise,
They, this thing, and I, that: whom shall my soul believe?

23.

Not on the vulgar mass
Called "work," must sentence pass,
Things done, that took the eye and had the price;
O'er which, from level stand,
The low world laid its hand,
Found straightway to its mind, could value in a trice:

24.

But all, the world's coarse thumb
And finger failed to plumb,
So passed in making up the main account;
All instincts immature,
All purposes unsure,
That weighed not as his work, yet swelled the man's amount:

25.

Thoughts hardly to be packed
Into a narrow act,
Fancies that broke through language and escaped;
All I could never be,
All, men ignored in me,
This, I was worth to God, whose wheel the pitcher shaped.

26.

Ay, note that Potter's wheel,
That metaphor! and feel
Why time spins fast, why passive lies our clay,—
Thou, to whom fools propound,
When the wine makes its round,
"Since life fleets, all is change; the Past gone, seize to-day!"

27.

Fool! All that is, at all,
Lasts ever, past recall;
Earth changes, but thy soul and God stand sure:
What entered into thee,
That was, is, and shall be:
Time's wheel runs back or stops; Potter and clay
 endure.

28.

He fixed thee mid this dance
Of plastic circumstance,
This Present, thou, forsooth, wouldst fain arrest:
Machinery just meant
To give thy soul its bent,
Try thee and turn thee forth, sufficiently impressed.

29.

What though the earlier grooves
Which ran the laughing loves
Around thy base, no longer pause and press?
What though, about thy rim,
Scull-things in order grim
Grow out, in graver mood, obey the sterner stress?

30.

Look not thou down but up!
To uses of a cup,
The festal board, lamp's flash and trumpet's peal,
The new wine's foaming flow,
The Master's lips a-glow!
Thou, heaven's consummate cup, what needst thou with earth's wheel?

31.

But I need, now as then,
Thee, God, who mouldest men;
And since, not even while the whirl was worst,
Did I,—to the wheel of life
With shapes and colours rife,
Bound dizzily,—mistake my end, to slake Thy thirst:

32.

So, take and use Thy work!
Amend what flaws may lurk,
What strain o' the stuff, what warpings past the aim!
My times be in Thy hand!
Perfect the cup as planned!
Let age approve of youth, and death complete the same!

A DEATH IN THE DESERT.

A DEATH IN THE DESERT.

[SUPPOSED of Pamphylax the Antiochene:
It is a parchment, of my rolls the fifth,
Hath three skins glued together, is all Greek,
And goeth from *Epsilon* down to *Mu*:
Lies second in the surnamed Chosen Chest,
Stained and conserved with juice of terebinth,
Covered with cloth of hair, and lettered *Xi*,
From Xanthus, my wife's uncle, now at peace:
Mu and *Epsilon* stand for my own name,
I may not write it, but I make a cross
To show I wait His coming, with the rest,
And leave off here: beginneth Pamphylax.]

I said, "If one should wet his lips with wine,
And slip the broadest plantain-leaf we find,
Or else the lappet of a linen robe,
Into the water-vessel, lay it right,
And cool his forehead just above the eyes,
The while a brother, kneeling either side,
Should chafe each hand and try to make it warm,—
He is not so far gone but he might speak."

This did not happen in the outer cave,
Nor in the secret chamber of the rock,
Where, sixty days since the decree was out,
We had him, bedded on a camel-skin,
And waited for his dying all the while;
But in the midmost grotto: since noon's light
Reached there a little, and we would not lose
The last of what might happen on his face.

I at the head, and Xanthus at the feet,
With Valens and the Boy, had lifted him,
And brought him from the chamber in the depths,
And laid him in the light where we might see:
For certain smiles began about his mouth,
And his lids moved, presageful of the end.

Beyond, and half way up the mouth o' the cave,
The Bactrian convert, having his desire,

Kept watch, and made pretence to graze a goat
That gave us milk, on rags of various herb,
Plantain and quitch, the rocks' shade keeps alive:
So that if any thief or soldier passed,
(Because the persecution was aware)
Yielding the goat up promptly with his life,
Such man might pass on, joyful at a prize,
Nor care to pry into the cool o' the cave.
Outside was all noon and the burning blue.

"Here is wine," answered Xanthus,—dropped a drop;
I stooped and placed the lap of cloth aright,
Then chafed his right hand, and the Boy his left:
But Valens had bethought him, and produced
And broke a ball of nard, and made perfume.
Only, he did—not so much wake, as—turn
And smile a little, as a sleeper does
If any dear one call him, touch his face—
And smiles and loves, but will not be disturbed.

Then Xanthus said a prayer, but still he slept:
It is the Xanthus that escaped to Rome,
Was burned, and could not write the chronicle.

Then the Boy sprang up from his knees, and ran,
Stung by the splendour of a sudden thought,

And fetched the seventh plate of graven lead
Out of the secret chamber, found a place,
Pressing with finger on the deeper dints,
And spoke, as 'twere his mouth proclaiming first,
"I am the Resurrection and the Life."

Whereat he opened his eyes wide at once,
And sat up of himself, and looked at us;
And thenceforth nobody pronounced a word:
Only, outside, the Bactrian cried his cry
Like the lone desert-bird that wears the ruff,
As signal we were safe, from time to time.

First he said, "If a friend declared to me,
This my son Valens, this my other son,
Were James and Peter,—nay, declared as well
This lad was very John,—I could believe!
—Could, for a moment, doubtlessly believe:
So is myself withdrawn into my depths,
The soul retreated from the perished brain
Whence it was wont to feel and use the world
Through these dull members, done with long ago.
Yet I myself remain; I feel myself:
And there is nothing lost. · Let be, awhile!"

[This is the doctrine he was wont to teach,
How divers persons witness in each man,

Three souls which make up one soul: first, to wit,
A soul of each and all the bodily parts,
Seated therein, which works, and is what Does,
And has the use of earth, and ends the man
Downward: but, tending upward for advice,
Grows into, and again is grown into
By the next soul, which, seated in the brain,
Useth the first with its collected use,
And feeleth, thinketh, willeth,—is what Knows:
Which, duly tending upward in its turn,
Grows into, and again is grown into
By the last soul, that uses both the first,
Subsisting whether they assist or no,
And, constituting man's self, is what Is—
And leans upon the former, makes it play,
As that played off the first: and, tending up,
Holds, is upheld by, God, and ends the man
Upward in that dread point of intercourse,
Nor needs a place, for it returns to Him.
What Does, what Knows, what Is; three souls, one
    man.
I give the glossa of Theotypas.]

And then, "A stick, once fire from end to end;
Now, ashes save the tip that holds a spark!
Yet, blow the spark, it runs back, spreads itself

A little where the fire was: thus I urge
The soul that served me, till it task once more
What ashes of my brain have kept their shape,
And these make effort on the last o' the flesh,
Trying to taste again the truth of things—"
(He smiled)—"their very superficial truth;
As that ye are my sons, that it is long
Since James and Peter had release by death,
And I am only he, your brother John,
Who saw and heard, and could remember all.
Remember all! It is not much to say.
What if the truth broke on me from above
As once and oft-times? Such might hap again:
Doubtlessly He might stand in presence here,
With head wool-white, eyes flame, and feet like brass,
The sword and the seven stars, as I have seen—
I who now shudder only and surmise
'How did your brother bear that sight and live?'

"If I live yet, it is for good, more love
Through me to men: be nought but ashes here
That keep awhile my semblance, who was John,—
Still, when they scatter, there is left on earth
No one alive who knew (consider this!)
—Saw with his eyes and handled with his hands
That which was from the first, the Word of Life.
How will it be when none more saith 'I saw?'

"Such ever was love's way: to rise, it stoops.
Since I, whom Christ's mouth taught, was bidden
    teach,
I went, for many years, about the world,
Saying 'It was so; so I heard and saw,'
Speaking as the case asked: and men believed.
Afterward came the message to myself
In Patmos isle; I was not bidden teach,
But simply listen, take a book and write,
Nor set down other than the given word,
With nothing left to my arbitrament
To choose or change: I wrote, and men believed.
Then, for my time grew brief, no message more,
No call to write again, I found a way,
And, reasoning from my knowledge, merely taught
Men should, for love's sake, in love's strength, believe;
Or I would pen a letter to a friend
And urge the same as friend, nor less nor more:
Friends said I reasoned rightly, and believed.
But at the last, why, I seemed left alive
Like a sea-jelly weak on Patmos strand,
To tell dry sea-beach gazers how I fared
When there was mid-sea, and the mighty things;
Left to repeat, 'I saw, I heard, I knew,'
And go all over the old ground again,
With Antichrist already in the world,

And many Antichrists, who answered prompt
'Am I not Jasper as thyself art John?
Nay, young, whereas through age thou mayest forget:
Wherefore, explain, or how shall we believe?'
I never thought to call down fire on such,
Or, as in wonderful and early days,
Pick up the scorpion, tread the serpent dumb;
But patient stated much of the Lord's life
Forgotten or misdelivered, and let it work:
Since much that at the first, in deed and word,
Lay simply and sufficiently exposed,
Had grown (or else my soul was grown to match,
Fed through such years, familiar with such light,
Guarded and guided still to see and speak)
Of new significance and fresh result;
What first were guessed as points, I now knew stars,
And named them in the Gospel I have writ.
For men said, 'It is getting long ago:'
'Where is the promise of His coming?'—asked
These young ones in their strength, as loth to wait,
Of me who, when their sires were born, was old.
I, for I loved them, answered, joyfully,
Since I was there, and helpful in my age;
And, in the main, I think such men believed.
Finally, thus endeavouring, I fell sick,
Ye brought me here, and I supposed the end,

And went to sleep with one thought that, at least,
Though the whole earth should lie in wickedness,
We had the truth, might leave the rest to God.
Yet now I wake in such decrepitude
As I had slidden down and fallen afar,
Past even the presence of my former self,
Grasping the while for stay at facts which snap,
Till I am found away from my own world,
Feeling for foot-hold through a blank profound,
Along with unborn people in strange lands,
Who say—I hear said or conceive they say—
'Was John at all, and did he say he saw?
Assure us, ere we ask what he might see!'

"And how shall I assure them?   Can they share
—They, who have flesh, a veil of youth and strength
About each spirit, that needs must bide its time,
Living and learning still as years assist
Which wear the thickness thin, and let man see—
With me who hardly am withheld at all,
But shudderingly, scarce a shred between,
Lie bare to the universal prick of light?
Is it for nothing we grow old and weak,
We whom God loves?   When pain ends, gain ends too.
To me, that story—ay, that Life and Death
Of which I wrote 'it was'—to me, it is;

—Is, here and now: I apprehend nought else.
Is not God now i' the world His power first made?
Is not His love at issue still with sin,
Closed with and cast and conquered, crucified
Visibly when a wrong is done on earth?
Love, wrong, and pain, what see I else around?
Yea, and the Resurrection and Uprise
To the right hand of the throne—what is it beside,
When such truth, breaking bounds, o'erfloods my soul,
And, as I saw the sin and death, even so
See I the need yet transiency of both,
The good and glory consummated thence?
I saw the Power; I see the Love, once weak,
Resume the Power: and in this word 'I see,'
Lo, there is recognized the Spirit of both
That, moving o'er the spirit of man, unblinds
His eye and bids him look. These are, I see;
But ye, the children, His beloved ones too,
Ye need,—as I should use an optic glass
I wondered at erewhile, somewhere i' the world,
It had been given a crafty smith to make;
A tube, he turned on objects brought too close,
Lying confusedly insubordinate
For the unassisted eye to master once:
Look through his tube, at distance now they lay,
Become succinct, distinct, so small, so clear!

Just thus, ye needs must apprehend what truth
I see, reduced to plain historic fact,
Diminished into clearness, proved a point
And far away: ye would withdraw your sense
From out eternity, strain it upon time,
Then stand before that fact, that Life and Death,
Stay there at gaze, till it dispart, dispread,
As though a star should open out, all sides,
And grow the world on you, as it is my world.

" For life, with all it yields of joy and woe,
And hope and fear,—believe the aged friend,—
Is just our chance o' the prize of learning love,
How love might be, hath been indeed, and is;
And that we hold thenceforth to the uttermost
Such prize despite the envy of the world,
And, having gained truth, keep truth: that is all.
But see the double way wherein we are led,
How the soul learns diversely from the flesh!
With flesh, that hath so little time to stay,
And yields mere basement for the soul's emprise,
Expect prompt teaching. Helpful was the light,
And warmth was cherishing and food was choice
To every man's flesh, thousand years ago,
As now to yours and mine; the body sprang
At once to the height, and stayed: but the soul,—no!

Since sages who, this noontide, meditate
In Rome or Athens, may descry some point
Of the eternal power, hid yestereve;
And as thereby the power's whole mass extends,
So much extends the æther floating o'er,
The love that tops the might, the Christ in God.
Then, as new lessons shall be learned in these
Till earth's work stop and useless time run out,
So duly, daily, needs provision be
For keeping the soul's prowess possible,
Building new barriers as the old decay,
Saving us from evasion of life's proof,
Putting the question ever, 'Does God love,
And will ye hold that truth against the world?'
Ye know there needs no second proof with good
Gained for our flesh from any earthly source:
We might go freezing, ages,—give us fire,
Thereafter we judge fire at its full worth,
And guard it safe through every chance, ye know!
That fable of Prometheus and his theft,
How mortals gained Jove's fiery flower, grows old
(I have been used to hear the pagans own)
And out of mind; but fire, howe'er its birth,
Here is it, precious to the sophist now
Who laughs the myth of Æschylus to scorn,
As precious to those satyrs of his play,

Who touched it in gay wonder at the thing.
While were it so with the soul,—this gift of truth
Once grasped, were this our soul's gain safe, and sure
To prosper as the body's gain is wont,—
Why, man's probation would conclude, his earth
Crumble; for he both reasons and decides,
Weighs first, then chooses: will he give up fire
For gold or purple once he knows its worth?
Could he give Christ up were His worth as plain?
Therefore, I say, to test man, shift the proofs,
Nor may he grasp that fact like other fact,
And straightway in his life acknowledge it,
As, say, the indubitable bliss of fire.
Sigh ye, 'It had been easier once than now?'
To give you answer I am left alive;
Look at me who was present from the first!
Ye know what things I saw; then came a test,
My first, befitting me who so had seen:
'Forsake the Christ thou sawest transfigured, Him
Who trod the sea and brought the dead to life?
What should wring this from thee?'—ye laugh and ask.
What wrung it? Even a torchlight and a noise,
The sudden Roman faces, violent hands,
And fear of what the Jews might do! Just that,
And, it is written, 'I forsook and fled':
There was my trial, and it ended thus.

Ay, but my soul had gained its truth, could grow:
Another year or two,—what little child,
What tender woman that had seen no least
Of all my sights, but barely heard them told,
Who did not clasp the cross with a light laugh,
Or wrap the burning robe round, thanking God?
Well, was truth safe for ever, then? Not so.
Already had begun the silent work
Whereby truth, deadened of its absolute blaze,
Might need love's eye to pierce the o'erstretched
    doubt:
Teachers were busy, whispering 'All is true
As the aged ones report; but youth can reach
Where age gropes dimly, weak with stir and strain,
And the full doctrine slumbers till to-day.'
Thus, what the Roman's lowered spear was found,
A bar to me who touched and handled truth,
Now proved the glozing of some new shrewd tongue,
This Ebion, this Cerinthus or their mates,
Till imminent was the outcry 'Save us Christ!'
Whereon I stated much of the Lord's life
Forgotten or misdelivered, and let it work.
Such work done, as it will be, what comes next?
What do I hear say, or conceive men say,
'Was John at all, and did he say he saw?
Assure us, ere we ask what he might see!'

"Is this indeed a burthen for late days,
And may I help to bear it with you all,
Using my weakness which becomes your strength?
For if a babe were born inside this grot,
Grew to a boy here, heard us praise the sun,
Yet had but yon sole glimmer in light's place,—
One loving him and wishful he should learn,
Would much rejoice himself was blinded first
Month by month here, so made to understand
How eyes, born darkling, apprehend amiss:
I think I could explain to such a child
There was more glow outside than gleams he caught,
Ay, nor need urge 'I saw it, so believe!'
It is a heavy burthen you shall bear
In latter days, new lands, or old grown strange,
Left without me, which must be very soon.
What is the doubt, my brothers? Quick with it!
I see you stand conversing, each new face,
Either in fields, of yellow summer eves,
On islets yet unnamed amid the sea;
Or pace for shelter 'neath a portico
Out of the crowd in some enormous town
Where now the larks sing in a solitude;
Or muse upon blank heaps of stone and sand
Idly conjectured to be Ephesus:
And no one asks his fellow any more

'Where is the promise of His coming?' but
'Was He revealed in any of His lives,
As Power, as Love, as Influencing Soul?'

"Quick, for time presses, tell the whole mind out,
And let us ask and answer and be saved!
My book speaks on, because it cannot pass;
One listens quietly, nor scoffs but pleads
'Here is a tale of things done ages since;
What truth was ever told the second day?
Wonders, that would prove doctrine, go for nought.
Remains the doctrine, love; well, we must love,
And what we love most, power and love in one,
Let us acknowledge on the record here,
Accepting these in Christ: must Christ then be?
Has He been? Did not we ourselves make Him?
Our mind receives but what it holds, no more.
First of the love, then; we acknowledge Christ—
A proof we comprehend His love, a proof .
We had such love already in ourselves,
Knew first what else we should not recognize.
'Tis mere projection from man's inmost mind,
And, what he loves, thus falls reflected back,
Becomes accounted somewhat out of him;
He throws it up in air, it drops down earth's,
With shape, name, story added, man's old way.

How prove you Christ came otherwise at least?
Next try the power: He made and rules the world:
Certes there is a world once made, now ruled,
Unless things have been ever as we see.
Our sires declared a charioteer's yoked steeds
Brought the sun up the east and down the west,
Which only of itself now rises, sets,
As if a hand impelled it and a will,—
Thus they long thought, they who had will and hands:
But the new question's whisper is distinct,
' Wherefore must all force needs be like ourselves?
We have the hands, the will; what made and drives
The sun is force, is law, is named, not known,
While will and love we do know; marks of these,
Eye-witnesses attest, so books declare—
As that, to punish or reward our race,
The sun at undue times arose or set
Or else stood still: what do not men affirm?
But earth requires as urgently reward
Or punishment to-day as years ago,
And none expects the sun will interpose:
Therefore it was mere passion and mistake,
Or erring zeal for right, which changed the truth.
Go back, far, farther, to the birth of things;
Ever the will, the intelligence, the love,
Man's!—which he gives, supposing he but finds,

As late he gave head, body, hands and feet,
To help these in what forms he called his gods.
First, Jove's brow, Juno's eyes were swept away,
But Jove's wrath, Juno's pride continued long;
As last, will, power, and love discarded these,
So law in turn discards power, love, and will.
What proveth God is otherwise at least?
All else, projection from the mind of man!'

"Nay, do not give me wine, for I am strong,
But place my gospel where I put my hands.

"I say that man was made to grow, not stop;
That help, he needed once, and needs no more,
Having grown up but an inch by, is withdrawn:
For he hath new needs, and new helps to these.
This imports solely, man should mount on each
New height in view; the help whereby he mounts,
The ladder-rung his foot has left, may fall,
Since all things suffer change save God the Truth.
Man apprehends Him newly at each stage
Whereat earth's ladder drops, its service done;
And nothing shall prove twice what once was proved.
You stick a garden-plot with ordered twigs
To show inside lie germs of herbs unborn,
And check the careless step would spoil their birth;
But when herbs wave, the guardian twigs may go,

Since should ye doubt of virtues, question kinds,
It is no longer for old twigs ye look,
Which proved once underneath lay store of seed,
But to the herb's self, by what light ye boast,
For what fruit's signs are. This book's fruit is
    plain,
Nor miracles need prove it any more.
Doth the fruit show? Then miracles bade 'ware
At first of root and stem, saved both till now
From trampling ox, rough boar and wanton goat.
What? Was man made a wheelwork to wind up,
And be discharged, and straight wound up anew?
No!—grown, his growth lasts; taught, he ne'er
    forgets:
May learn a thousand things, not twice the same.

" This might be pagan teaching: now hear mine.

" I say, that as the babe, you feed awhile,
Becomes a boy and fit to feed himself,
So, minds at first must be spoon-fed with truth:
When they can eat, babe's nurture is withdrawn.
I fed the babe whether it would or no:
I bid the boy or feed himself or starve.
I cried once, ' That ye may believe in Christ,
Behold this blind man shall receive his sight!'
I cry now, ' Urgest thou, *for I am shrewd*

And smile at stories how John's word could cure—
Repeat that miracle and take my faith?
I say, that miracle was duly wrought
When, save for it, no faith was possible.
Whether a change were wrought i' the shows o' the
    world,
Whether the change came from our minds which see
Of the shows o' the world so much as and no more
Than God wills for His purpose,—(what do I
See now, suppose you, there where you see rock
Round us?)—I know not; such was the effect,
So faith grew, making void more miracles
Because too much: they would compel, not help.
I say, the acknowledgment of God in Christ
Accepted by thy reason, solves for thee
All questions in the earth and out of it,
And has so far advanced thee to be wise.
Wouldst thou unprove this to re-prove the proved?
In life's mere minute, with power to use that proof,
Leave knowledge and revert to how it sprung?
Thou hast it; use it and forthwith, or die!

" For I say, this is death and the sole death,
When a man's loss comes to him from his gain,
Darkness from light, from knowledge ignorance,
And lack of love from love made manifest;

A lamp's death when, replete with oil, it chokes;
A stomach's when, surcharged with food, it starves.
With ignorance was surety of a cure.
When man, appalled at nature, questioned first
'What if there lurk a might behind this might?'
He needed satisfaction God could give,
And did give, as ye have the written word:
But when he finds might still redouble might,
Yet asks, 'Since all is might, what use of will?'
—Will, the one source of might,—he being man
With a man's will and a man's might, to teach
In little how the two combine in large,—
That man has turned round on himself and stands,
Which in the course of nature is, to die.

" And when man questioned, 'What if there be
    love
Behind the will and might, as real as they?'—
He needed satisfaction God could give,
And did give, as ye have the written word:
But when, beholding that love everywhere,
He reasons, 'Since such love is everywhere,
And since ourselves can love and would be loved,
We ourselves make the love, and Christ was not,'—
How shall ye help this man who knows himself,
That he must love and would be loved again,

Yet, owning his own love that proveth Christ,
Rejecteth Christ through very need of Him?
The lamp o'erswims with oil, the stomach flags
Loaded with nurture, and that man's soul dies.

"If he rejoin, 'But this was all the while
A trick; the fault was, first of all, in thee,
Thy story of the places, names and dates,
Where, when and how the ultimate truth had rise,
—Thy prior truth, at last discovered none,
Whence now the second suffers detriment.
What good of giving knowledge if, because
Of the manner of the gift, its profit fail?
And why refuse what modicum of help
Had stopped the after-doubt, impossible
I' the face of truth—truth absolute, uniform?
Why must I hit of this and miss of that,
Distinguish just as I be weak or strong,
And not ask of thee and have answer prompt,
Was this once, was it not once?—then and now
And evermore, plain truth from man to man.
Is John's procedure just the heathen bard's?
Put question of his famous play again
How for the ephemerals' sake, Jove's fire was filched,
And carried in a cane and brought to earth:
The fact is in the fable, cry the wise,

*Mortals obtained the boon, so much is fact,
Though fire be spirit and produced on earth.
As with the Titan's, so now with thy tale:
Why breed in us perplexity, mistake,
Nor tell the whole truth in the proper words?'*

"I answer, Have ye yet to argue out
The very primal thesis, plainest law,
— Man is not God but hath God's end to serve,
A master to obey, a course to take,
Somewhat to cast off, somewhat to become?
Grant this, then man must pass from old to new,
From vain to real, from mistake to fact,
From what once seemed good, to what now proves
    best.
How could man have progression otherwise?
Before the point was mooted 'What is God?'
No savage man inquired 'What am myself?'
Much less replied, 'First, last, and best of
    things.'
Man takes that title now if he believes
Might can exist with neither will nor love,
In God's case—what he names now Nature's Law—
While in himself he recognizes love
No less than might and will: and rightly takes.
Since if man prove the sole existent thing

I

Where these combine, whatever their degree,
However weak the might or will or love,
So they be found there, put in evidence,—
He is as surely higher in the scale
Than any might with neither love nor will,
As life, apparent in the poorest midge,
When the faint dust-speck flits, ye guess its wing,
Is marvellous beyond dead Atlas' self:
I give such to the midge for resting-place!
Thus, man proves best and highest—God, in fine,
And thus the victory leads but to defeat,
The gain to loss, best rise to the worst fall,
His life becomes impossible, which is death.

" But if, appealing thence, he cower, avouch
He is mere man, and in humility
Neither may know God nor mistake himself;
I point to the immediate consequence
And say, by such confession straight he falls
Into man's place, a thing nor God nor beast,
Made to know that he can know and not more:
Lower than God who knows all and can all,
Higher than beasts which know and can so far
As each beast's limit, perfect to an end,
Nor conscious that they know, nor craving more;
While man knows partly but conceives beside,

Creeps ever on from fancies to the fact,
And in this striving, this converting air
Into a solid he may grasp and use,
Finds progress, man's distinctive mark alone,
Not God's, and not the beasts': God is, they are,
Man partly is and wholly hopes to be.
Such progress could no more attend his soul
Were all it struggles after found at first
And guesses changed to knowledge absolute,
Than motion wait his body, were all else
Than it the solid earth on every side,
Where now through space he moves from rest to rest.
Man, therefore, thus conditioned, must expect
He could not, what he knows now, know at first;
What he considers that he knows to-day,
Come but to-morrow, he will find misknown;
Getting increase of knowledge, since he learns
Because he lives, which is to be a man,
Set to instruct himself by his past self:
First, like the brute, obliged by facts to learn,
Next, as man may, obliged by his own mind,
Bent, habit, nature, knowledge turned to law.
God's gift was that man should conceive of truth
And yearn to gain it, catching at mistake,
As midway help till he reach fact indeed.
The statuary ere he mould a shape

Boasts a like gift, the shape's idea, and next
The aspiration to produce the same;
So, taking clay, he calls his shape thereout,
Cries ever 'Now I have the thing I see':
Yet all the while goes changing what was wrought,
From falsehood like the truth, to truth itself.
How were it had he cried 'I see no face,
No breast, no feet i' the ineffectual clay?'
Rather commend him that he clapped his hands,
And laughed 'It is my shape and lives again!'
Enjoyed the falsehood, touched it on to truth,
Until yourselves applaud the flesh indeed
In what is still flesh-imitating clay.
Right in you, right in him, such way be man's!
God only makes the live shape at a jet.
Will ye renounce this pact of creatureship?
The pattern on the Mount subsists no more,
Seemed awhile, then returned to nothingness;
But copies, Moses strove to make thereby,
Serve still and are replaced as time requires:
By these, make newest vessels, reach the type!
If ye demur, this judgment on your head,
Never to reach the ultimate, angels' law,
Indulging every instinct of the soul
There where law, life, joy, impulse are one thing!

"Such is the burthen of the latest time.
I have survived to hear it with my ears,
Answer it with my lips: does this suffice?
For if there be a further woe than such,
Wherein my brothers struggling need a hand,
So long as any pulse is left in mine,
May I be absent even longer yet,
Plucking the blind ones back from the abyss,
Though I should tarry a new hundred years!"

But he was dead: 'twas about noon, the day
Somewhat declining: we five buried him
That eve, and then, dividing, went five ways,
And I, disguised, returned to Ephesus.

By this, the cave's mouth must be filled with sand.
Valens is lost, I know not of his trace;
The Bactrian was but a wild, childish man,
And could not write nor speak, but only loved:
So, lest the memory of this go quite,
Seeing that I to-morrow fight the beasts,
I tell the same to Phœbas, whom believe!
For many look again to find that face,
Beloved John's to whom I ministered,
Somewhere in life about the world; they err:
Either mistaking what was darkly spoke
At ending of his book, as he relates,

Or misconceiving somewhat of this speech
Scattered from mouth to mouth, as I suppose.
Believe ye will not see him any more
About the world with his divine regard!
For all was as I say, and now the man
Lies as he lay once, breast to breast with God.

[Cerinthus read and mused; one added this:

"If Christ, as thou affirmest, be of men
Mere man, the first and best but nothing more,—
Account Him, for reward of what He was,
Now and for ever, wretchedest of all.
For see; Himself conceived of life as love,
Conceived of love as what must enter in,
Fill up, make one with His each soul He loved:
Thus much for man's joy, all men's joy for Him.
Well, He is gone, thou sayest, to fit reward.
But by this time are many souls set free,
And very many still retained alive:
Nay, should His coming be delayed awhile,
Say, ten years longer (twelve years, some compute)
See if, for every finger of thy hands,
There be not found, that day the world shall end,
Hundreds of souls, each holding by Christ's word
That He will grow incorporate with all,

With me as Pamphylax, with him as John,
Groom for each bride! Can a mere man do this?
Yet Christ saith, this He lived and died to do.
Call Christ, then, the illimitable God,
Or lost!"

        But 'twas Cerinthus that is lost.]

CALIBAN UPON SETEBOS;

OR,

NATURAL THEOLOGY IN THE ISLAND.

———

"Thou thoughtest that I was altogether such an one as thyself."

CALIBAN UPON SETEBOS;

OR,

NATURAL THEOLOGY IN THE ISLAND.

['WILL sprawl, now that the heat of day is best,
Flat on his belly in the pit's much mire,
With elbows wide, fists clenched to prop his chin;
And, while he kicks both feet in the cool slush,
And feels about his spine small eft-things course,
Run in and out each arm, and make him laugh;
And while above his head a pompion-plant,
Coating the cave-top as a brow its eye,
Creeps down to touch and tickle hair and beard,
And now a flower drops with a bee inside,
And now a fruit to snap at, catch and crunch:
He looks out o'er yon sea which sunbeams cross

And recross till they weave a spider-web,
(Meshes of fire, some great fish breaks at times)
And talks to his own self, howe'er he please,
Touching that other, whom his dam called God.
Because to talk about Him, vexes—ha,
Could He but know! and time to vex is now,
When talk is safer than in winter-time.
Moreover Prosper and Miranda sleep
In confidence he drudges at their task,
And it is good to cheat the pair, and gibe,
Letting the rank tongue blossom into speech.]

Setebos, Setebos, and Setebos!
'Thinketh, He dwelleth i' the cold o' the moon.

'Thinketh He made it, with the sun to match,
But not the stars; the stars came otherwise;
Only made clouds, winds, meteors, such as that:
Also this isle, what lives and grows thereon,
And snaky sea which rounds and ends the same.

'Thinketh, it came of being ill at ease:
He hated that He cannot change His cold,
Nor cure its ache. 'Hath spied an icy fish
That longed to 'scape the rock-stream where she lived,
And thaw herself within the lukewarm brine

O' the lazy sea her stream thrusts far amid,
A crystal spike 'twixt two warm walls of wave;
Only she ever sickened, found repulse
At the other kind of water, not her life,
(Green-dense and dim-delicious, bred o' the sun)
Flounced back from bliss she was not born to breathe,
And in her old bounds buried her despair,
Hating and loving warmth alike: so He.

'Thinketh, He made thereat the sun, this isle,
Trees and the fowls here, beast and creeping thing.
Yon otter, sleek-wet, black, lithe as a leech;
Yon auk, one fire-eye in a ball of foam,
That floats and feeds; a certain badger brown
He hath watched hunt with that slant white-wedge eye
By moonlight; and the pie with the long tongue
That pricks deep into oakwarts for a worm,
And says a plain word when she finds her prize,
But will not eat the ants; the ants themselves
That build a wall of seeds and settled stalks
About their hole—He made all these and more,
Made all we see, and us, in spite: how else?
He could not, Himself, make a second self
To be His mate; as well have made Himself.
He would not make what He mislikes or slights,
An eyesore to Him, or not worth His pains:

But did, in envy, listlessness or sport,
Make what Himself would fain, in a manner, be—
Weaker in most points, stronger in a few,
Worthy, and yet mere playthings all the while,
Things He admires and mocks too,—that is it.
Because, so brave, so better though they be,
It nothing skills if He begin to plague.
Look now, I melt a gourd-fruit into mash,
Add honeycomb and pods, I have perceived,
Which bite like finches when they bill and kiss,—
Then, when froth rises bladdery, drink up all,
Quick, quick, till maggots scamper through my brain;
And throw me on my back i' the seeded thyme,
And wanton, wishing I were born a bird.
Put case, unable to be what I wish,
I yet could make a live bird out of clay:
Would not I take clay, pinch my Caliban
Able to fly?—for, there, see, he hath wings,
And great comb like the hoopoe's to admire,
And there, a sting to do his foes offence,
There, and I will that he begin to live,
Fly to yon rock-top, nip me off the horns
Of grigs high up that make the merry din,
Saucy through their veined wings, and mind me not.
In which feat, if his leg snapped, brittle clay,
And he lay stupid-like,—why, I should laugh;

And if he, spying me, should fall to weep,
Beseech me to be good, repair his wrong,
Bid his poor leg smart less or grow again,—
Well, as the chance were, this might take or else
Not take my fancy: I might hear his cry,
And give the manikin three legs for his one,
Or pluck the other off, leave him like an egg,
And lessoned he was mine and merely clay.
Were this no pleasure, lying in the thyme,
Drinking the mash, with brain become alive,
Making and marring clay at will? So He.

'Thinketh, such shows nor right nor wrong in Him,
Nor kind, nor cruel: He is strong and Lord.
'Am strong myself compared to yonder crabs
That march now from the mountain to the sea;
'Let twenty pass, and stone the twenty-first,
Loving not, hating not, just choosing so.
'Say, the first straggler that boasts purple spots
Shall join the file, one pincer twisted off;
'Say, this bruised fellow shall receive a worm,
And two worms he whose nippers end in red;
As it likes me each time, I do: so He.

Well then, 'supposeth He is good i' the main,
Placable if His mind and ways were guessed,

But rougher than His handiwork, be sure!
Oh, He hath made things worthier than Himself,
And envieth that, so helped, such things do more
Than He who made them! What consoles but this?
That they, unless through Him, do nought at all,
And must submit: what other use in things?
'Hath cut a pipe of pithless elder-joint
That, blown through, gives exact the scream o' the jay
When from her wing you twitch the feathers blue:
Sound this, and little birds that hate the jay
Flock within stone's throw, glad their foe is hurt:
Put case such pipe could prattle and boast forsooth
"I catch the birds, I am the crafty thing,
I make the cry my maker cannot make
With his great round mouth; he must blow through
   mine!"
Would not I smash it with my foot? So He.

But wherefore rough, why cold and ill at ease?
Aha, that is a question! Ask, for that,
What knows,—the something over Setebos
That made Him, or He, may be, found and fought,
Worsted, drove off and did to nothing, perchance.
There may be something quiet o'er His head,
Out of His reach, that feels nor joy nor grief,
Since both derive from weakness in some way.

I joy because the quails come; would not joy
Could I bring quails here when I have a mind:
This Quiet, all it hath a mind to, doth.
'Esteemeth stars the outposts of its couch,
But never spends much thought nor care that way.
It may look up, work up,—the worse for those
It works on! 'Careth but for Setebos
The many-handed as a cuttle-fish,
Who, making Himself feared through what He does,
Looks up, first, and perceives He cannot soar
To what is quiet and hath happy life;
Next looks down here, and out of very spite
Makes this a bauble-world to ape yon real,
These good things to match those as hips do grapes.
'Tis solace making baubles, ay, and sport.
Himself peeped late, eyed Prosper at his books
Careless and lofty, lord now of the isle:
Vexed, 'stitched a book of broad leaves, arrow-shaped,
Wrote thereon, he knows what, prodigious words;
Has peeled a wand and called it by a name;
Weareth at whiles for an enchanter's robe
The eyed skin of a supple oncelot;
And hath an ounce sleeker than youngling mole,
A four-legged serpent he makes cower and couch,
Now snarl, now hold its breath and mind his eye,
And saith she is Miranda and my wife:

'Keeps for his Ariel a tall pouch-bill crane
He bids go wade for fish and straight disgorge;
Also a sea-beast, lumpish, which he snared,
Blinded the eyes of, and brought somewhat tame,
And split its toe-webs, and now pens the drudge
In a hole o' the rock and calls him Caliban;
A bitter heart, that bides its time and bites.
'Plays thus at being Prosper in a way,
Taketh his mirth with make-believes: so He.

His dam held that the Quiet made all things
Which Setebos vexed only: 'holds not so.
Who made them weak, meant weakness He might vex.
Had He meant other, while His hand was in,
Why not make horny eyes no thorn could prick,
Or plate my scalp with bone against the snow,
Or overscale my flesh 'neath joint and joint,
Like an orc's armour? Ay,—so spoil His sport!
He is the One now: only He doth all.

'Saith, He may like, perchance, what profits Him.
Ay, himself loves what does him good; but why?
'Gets good no otherwise. This blinded beast
Loves whoso places flesh-meat on his nose,
But, had he eyes, would want no help, but hate
Or love, just as it liked him: He hath eyes.

Also it pleaseth Setebos to work,
Use all His hands, and exercise much craft,
By no means for the love of what is worked.
'Tasteth, himself, no finer good i' the world
When all goes right, in this safe summer-time,
And he wants little, hungers, aches not much,
Than trying what to do with wit and strength.
'Falls to make something: 'piled yon pile of turfs,
And squared and stuck there squares of soft white chalk,
And, with a fish-tooth, scratched a moon on each,
And set up endwise certain spikes of tree,
And crowned the whole with a sloth's skull a-top,
Found dead i' the woods, too hard for one to kill.
No use at all i' the work, for work's sole sake;
'Shall some day knock it down again: so He.

'Saith He is terrible: watch His feats in proof!
One hurricane will spoil six good months' hope.
He hath a spite against me, that I know,
Just as He favours Prosper, who knows why?
So it is, all the same, as well I find.
'Wove wattles half the winter, fenced them firm
With stone and stake to stop she-tortoises
Crawling to lay their eggs here: well, one wave,
Feeling the foot of Him upon its neck,

Gaped as a snake does, lolled out its large tongue,
And licked the whole labour flat: so much for spite.
'Saw a ball flame down late (yonder it lies)
Where, half an hour before, I slept i' the shade:
Often they scatter sparkles: there is force!
'Dug up a newt He may have envied once
And turned to stone, shut up inside a stone.
Please Him and hinder this?—What Prosper does?
Aha, if He would tell me how! Not He!
There is the sport: discover how or die!
All need not die, for of the things o' the isle
Some flee afar, some dive, some run up trees;
Those at His mercy,—why, they please Him most
When . . when . . well, never try the same way twice!
Repeat what act has pleased, He may grow wroth.
You must not know His ways, and play Him off,
Sure of the issue. 'Doth the like himself:
'Spareth a squirrel that it nothing fears
But steals the nut from underneath my thumb,
And when I threat, bites stoutly in defence:
'Spareth an urchin that, contrariwise,
Curls up into a ball, pretending death
For fright at my approach: the two ways please.
But what would move my choler more than this,
That either creature counted on its life
To-morrow and next day and all days to come,

Saying forsooth in the inmost of its heart,
" Because he did so yesterday with me,
And otherwise with such another brute,
So must he do henceforth and always."—Ay?
'Would teach the reasoning couple what "must" means!
'Doth as he likes, or wherefore Lord? So He.

'Conceiveth all things will continue thus,
And we shall have to live in fear of Him
So long as He lives, keeps His strength: no change,
If He have done His best, make no new world
To please Him more, so leave off watching this,—
If He surprise not even the Quiet's self
Some strange day,—or, suppose, grow into it
As grubs grow butterflies: else, here are we,
And there is He, and nowhere help at all.

'Believeth with the life, the pain shall stop.
His dam held different, that after death
He both plagued enemies and feasted friends:
Idly! He doth His worst in this our life,
Giving just respite lest we die through pain,
Saving last pain for worst,—with which, an end.
Meanwhile, the best way to escape His ire
Is, not to seem too happy. Sees, himself,
Yonder two flies, with purple films and pink,

Bask on the pompion-bell above : kills both.
'Sees two black painful beetles roll their ball
On head and tail as if to save their lives :
Moves them the stick away they strive to clear.

Even so, 'would have Him misconceive, suppose
This Caliban strives hard and ails no less,
And always, above all else, envies Him.
Wherefore he mainly dances on dark nights,
Moans in the sun, gets under holes to laugh,
And never speaks his mind save housed as now :
Outside, 'groans, curses. If He caught me here,
O'erheard this speech, and asked "What chucklest at?"
'Would, to appease Him, cut a finger off,
Or of my three kid yearlings burn the best,
Or let the toothsome apples rot on tree,
Or push my tame beast for the orc to taste :
While myself lit a fire, and made a song
And sung it, " *What I hate, be consecrate*
To celebrate Thee and Thy state, no mate
For Thee ; what see for envy in poor me ?"
Hoping the while, since evils sometimes mend,
Warts rub away, and sores are cured with slime,
That some strange day, will either the Quiet catch
And conquer Setebos, or likelier He
Decrepit may doze, doze, as good as die.

[What, what? A curtain o'er the world at once!
Crickets stop hissing; not a bird—or, yes,
There scuds His raven that hath told Him all!
It was fool's play, this prattling! Ha! The wind
Shoulders the pillared dust, death's house o' the move,
And fast invading fires begin! White blaze—
A tree's head snaps—and there, there, there, there, there,
His thunder follows! Fool to gibe at Him!
Lo! 'Lieth flat and loveth Setebos!
'Maketh his teeth meet through his upper lip,
Will let those quails fly, will not eat this month
One little mess of whelks, so he may 'scape!]

CONFESSIONS.

CONFESSIONS.

1.

WHAT is he buzzing in my ears?
   "Now that I come to die,
Do I view the world as a vale of tears?"
   Ah, reverend sir, not I!

2.

What I viewed there once, what I view again.
   Where the physic bottles stand
On the table's edge,—is a suburb lane,
   With a wall to my bedside hand.

3.

That lane sloped, much as the bottles do,
　From a house you could descry
O'er the garden-wall: is the curtain blue
　Or green to a healthy eye?

4.

To mine, it serves for the old June weather
　Blue above lane and wall;
And that farthest bottle labelled " Ether"
　Is the house o'er-topping all.

5.

At a terrace, somewhat near its stopper,
　There watched for me, one June,
A girl: I know, sir, it's improper,
　My poor mind's out of tune.

6.

Only, there was a way . . you crept
　Close by the side, to dodge
Eyes in the house, two eyes except:
　They styled their house " The Lodge."

7.

What right had a lounger up their lane?
    But, by creeping very close,
With the good wall's help,—their eyes might strain
    And stretch themselves to Oes,

8.

Yet never catch her and me together,
    As she left the attic, there,
By the rim of the bottle labelled " Ether,"
    And stole from stair to stair,

9.

And stood by the rose-wreathed gate. Alas,
    We loved, sir—used to meet:
How sad and bad and mad it was—
    But then, how it was sweet!

MAY AND DEATH.

MAY AND DEATH.

1.

I wish that when you died last May,
   Charles, there had died along with you
Three parts of spring's delightful things;
   Ay, and, for me, the fourth part too.

2.

A foolish thought, and worse, perhaps!
   There must be many a pair of friends
Who, arm in arm, deserve the warm
   Moon-births and the long evening-ends.

3.

So, for their sakes, be May still May!
    Let their new time, as mine of old,
Do all it did for me: I bid
    Sweet sights and sounds throng manifold.

4.

Only, one little sight, one plant,
    Woods have in May, that starts up green
Save a sole streak which, so to speak,
    Is spring's blood, spilt its leaves between,—

5.

That, they might spare; a certain wood
    Might miss the plant; their loss were small:
But I,—whene'er the leaf grows there,
    Its drop comes from my heart, that's all.

PROSPICE.

PROSPICE.

Fear death?—to feel the fog in my throat,
    The mist in my face,
When the snows begin, and the blasts denote
    I am nearing the place,
The power of the night, the press of the storm,
    The post of the foe;
Where he stands, the Arch Fear in a visible form,
    Yet the strong man must go:
For the journey is done and the summit attained,
    And the barriers fall,
Though a battle's to fight ere the guerdon be gained,
    The reward of it all.

I was ever a fighter, so—one fight more,
    The best and the last!
I would hate that death bandaged my eyes, and forbore,
    And bade me creep past.
No! let me taste the whole of it, fare like my peers
    The heroes of old,
Bear the brunt, in a minute pay glad life's arrears
    Of pain, darkness and cold.
For sudden the worst turns the best to the brave,
    The black minute's at end,
And the elements' rage, the fiend-voices that rave,
    Shall dwindle, shall blend,
Shall change, shall become first a peace, then a joy,
    Then a light, then thy breast,
O thou soul of my soul! I shall clasp thee again,
    And with God be the rest!

YOUTH AND ART.

YOUTH AND ART.

1.

It once might have been, once only:
    We lodged in a street together,
You, a sparrow on the housetop lonely,
    I, a lone she-bird of his feather.

2.

Your trade was with sticks and clay,
    You thumbed, thrust, patted and polished,
Then laughed "They will see some day
    Smith made, and Gibson demolished."

3.

My business was song, song, song;
    I chirped, cheeped, trilled and twittered,
"Kate Brown's on the boards ere long,
    And Grisi's existence embittered!"

4.

I earned no more by a warble
    Than you by a sketch in plaster;
You wanted a piece of marble,
    I needed a music-master.

5.

We studied hard in our styles,
    Chipped each at a crust like Hindoos,
For air, looked out on the tiles,
    For fun, watched each other's windows.

6.

You lounged, like a boy of the South,
    Cap and blouse—nay, a bit of beard too;
Or you got it, rubbing your mouth
    With fingers the clay adhered to.

7.

And I—soon managed to find
    Weak points in the flower-fence facing,
Was forced to put up a blind
    And be safe in my corset-lacing.

8.

No harm! It was not my fault
    If you never turned your eyes' tail up,
As I shook upon E *in alt.*,
    Or ran the chromatic scale up:

9.

For spring bade the sparrows pair,
    And the boys and girls gave guesses,
And stalls in our street looked rare
    With bulrush and watercresses.

10.

Why did not you pinch a flower
    In a pellet of clay and fling it?
Why did not I put a power
    Of thanks in a look, or sing it?

11.

I did look, sharp as a lynx,
  (And yet the memory rankles)
When models arrived, some minx
  Tripped up-stairs, she and her ankles.

12.

But I think I gave you as good!
  " That foreign fellow,—who can know
How she pays, in a playful mood,
  For his tuning her that piano?"

13.

Could you say so, and never say
  " Suppose we join hands and fortunes,
And I fetch her from over the way,
  Her, piano, and long tunes and short tunes?"

14.

No, no: you would not be rash,
  Nor I rasher and something over:
You 've to settle yet Gibson's hash,
  And Grisi yet lives in clover.

15.

But you meet the Prince at the Board,
   I 'm queen myself at *bals-paré*,
I 've married a rich old lord,
   And you 're dubbed knight and an R. A.

16.

Each life 's unfulfilled, you see ;
   It hangs still, patchy and scrappy :
We have not sighed deep, laughed free,
   Starved, feasted, despaired,—been happy.

17.

And nobody calls you a dunce,
   And people suppose me clever :
This could but have happened once,
   And we missed it, lost it for ever.

A FACE.

A FACE.

If one could have that little head of hers
Painted upon a background of pale gold,
Such as the Tuscan's early art prefers!
No shade encroaching on the matchless mould
Of those two lips, which should be opening soft
In the pure profile; not as when she laughs,
For that spoils all: but rather as if aloft
Yon hyacinth, she loves so, leaned its staff's
Burthen of honey-coloured buds to kiss
And capture 'twixt the lips apart for this.
Then her lithe neck, three fingers might surround,
How it should waver on the pale gold ground
Up to the fruit-shaped, perfect chin it lifts!

I know, Correggio loves to mass, in rifts
Of heaven, his angel faces, orb on orb
Breaking its outline, burning shades absorb:
But these are only massed there, I should think,
Waiting to see some wonder momently
Grow out, stand full, fade slow against the sky
(That's the pale ground you'd see this sweet face by),
All heaven, meanwhile, condensed into one eye
Which fears to lose the wonder, should it wink.

A LIKENESS.

A LIKENESS.

Some people hang portraits up
In a room where they dine or sup:
And the wife clinks tea-things under,
And her cousin, he stirs his cup,
Asks, " Who was the lady, I wonder?"
" 'Tis a daub John bought at a sale,"
Quoth the wife,—looks black as thunder:
" What a shade beneath her nose!
Snuff-taking, I suppose,—"
Adds the cousin, while John's corns ail.

Or else, there 's no wife in the case,
But the portrait 's queen of the place,

Alone mid the other spoils
Of youth,—masks, gloves and foils,
And pipe-sticks, rose, cherry-tree, jasmine,
And the long whip, the tandem-lasher,
And the cast from a fist (" not, alas! mine,
But my master's, the Tipton Slasher ")
And the cards where pistol-balls mark ace,
And a satin shoe used for cigar-case,
And the chamois-horns (" shot in the Chablais ")
And prints—Rarey drumming on Cruiser,
And Sayers, our champion, the bruiser,
And the little edition of Rabelais:
Where a friend, with both hands in his pockets,
May saunter up close to examine it,
And remark a good deal of Jane Lamb in it,
" But the eyes are half out of their sockets;
That hair's not so bad, where the gloss is,
But they've made the girl's nose a proboscis:
Jane Lamb, that we danced with at Vichy!
What, is not she Jane? Then, who is she?"

All that I own is a print,
An etching, a mezzotint;
'Tis a study, a fancy, a fiction,
Yet a fact (take my conviction)
Because it has more than a hint

A LIKENESS.

Of a certain face, I never
Saw elsewhere touch or trace of
In women I've seen the face of:
Just an etching, and, so far, clever.

I keep my prints, an imbroglio,
Fifty in one portfolio.
When somebody tries my claret,
We turn round chairs to the fire,
Chirp over days in a garret,
Chuckle o'er increase of salary,
Taste the good fruits of our leisure,
Talk about pencil and lyre,
And the National Portrait Gallery:
Then I exhibit my treasure.
After we've turned over twenty,
And the debt of wonder my crony owes
Is paid to my Marc Antonios,
He stops me—"*Festina lentè!*
What's that sweet thing there, the etching?"
How my waistcoat-strings want stretching,
How my cheeks grow red as tomatos,
How my heart leaps! But hearts, after leaps, ache.

" By the by, you must take, for a keepsake,
That other, you praised, of Volpato's."

The fool! would he try a flight further and say
He never saw, never before to-day,
What was able to take his breath away,
A face to lose youth for, to occupy age
With the dream of, meet death with,—why, I'll
  not engage
But that, half in a rapture and half in a rage,
I should toss him the thing's self—" 'Tis only a
  duplicate,
A thing of no value! Take it, I supplicate!"

MR. SLUDGE, "THE MEDIUM."

MR. SLUDGE, "THE MEDIUM."

Now, don't sir! Don't expose me! Just this once!
This was the first and only time, I'll swear,—
Look at me,—see, I kneel,—the only time,
I swear, I ever cheated,—yes, by the soul
Of Her who hears—(your sainted mother, sir!)
All, except this last accident, was truth—
This little kind of slip!—and even this,
It was your own wine, sir, the good champagne,
(I took it for Catawba,—you're so kind)
Which put the folly in my head!

                              "Get up?"
You still inflict on me that terrible face?
You show no mercy?—Not for Her dear sake,

The sainted spirit's, whose soft breath even now
Blows on my cheek—(don't you feel something, sir?)
You 'll tell?

          Go tell, then!   Who the devil cares
What such a rowdy chooses to . . .

                            Aie—aie—aie!
Please, sir! your thumbs are through my windpipe,
    sir!
Ch—ch!

          Well, sir, I hope you 've done it now!
Oh Lord! I little thought, sir, yesterday,
When your departed mother spoke those words
Of peace through me, and moved you, sir, so much,
You gave me—(very kind it was of you)
These shirt-studs—(better take them back again,
Please, sir!)—yes, little did I think so soon
A trifle of trick, all through a glass too much
Of his own champagne, would change my best of
    friends
Into an angry gentleman!

                    Though, 'twas wrong.
I don't contest the point; your anger 's just:

Whatever put such folly in my head,
I know 't was wicked of me.   There 's a thick,
Dusk, undeveloped spirit (I 've observed)
Owes me a grudge—a negro's, I should say,
Or else an Irish emigrant's ; yourself
Explained the case so well last Sunday, sir,
When we had summoned Franklin to clear up
A point about those shares in the telegraph :
Ay, and he swore . . or might it be Tom Paine ? . .
Thumping the table close by where I crouched,
He 'd do me soon a mischief: that 's come true !

Why, now your face clears ! I was sure it would !
Then, this one time . . don't take your hand away,
Through yours I surely kiss your mother's hand . .
You 'll promise to forgive me ?—or, at least,
Tell nobody of this ? Consider, sir !
What harm can mercy do ?   Would but the shade
Of the venerable dead-one just vouchsafe
A rap or tip !   What bit of paper 's here ?
Suppose we take a pencil, let her write,
Make the least sign, she urges on her child
Forgiveness ? There now ! Eh ? Oh ! 'Twas your
    foot,
And not a natural creak, sir ?

Answer, then!
Once, twice, thrice . . . see, I'm waiting to say
    "thrice!"
All to no use? No sort of hope for me?
It's all to post to Greeley's newspaper?

What? If I told you all about the tricks?
Upon my soul!—the whole truth, and nought else,
And how there's been some falsehood—for your part,
Will you engage to pay my passage out,
And hold your tongue until I'm safe on board?
England's the place, not Boston—no offence!
I see what makes you hesitate: don't fear!
I mean to change my trade and cheat no more,
Yes, this time really it's upon my soul!
Be my salvation!—under Heaven, of course.
I'll tell some queer things. Sixty Vs must do.
A trifle, though, to start with! We'll refer
The question to this table?

                        How you're changed!
Then split the difference; thirty more, we'll say.
Ay, but you leave my presents! Else I'll swear
'Twas all through those: you wanted yours again,
So, picked a quarrel with me, to get them back!
Tread on a worm, it turns, sir! If I turn,

Your fault! 'Tis you 'll have forced me! Who 's
    obliged
To give up life yet try no self-defence?
At all events, I 'll run the risk.   Eh?

                                  Done!
May I sit, sir? This dear old table, now!
Please, sir, a parting egg-nogg and cigar!
I 've been so happy with you! Nice stuffed chairs,
And sympathetic sideboards; what an end
To all the instructive evenings! (It 's alight.)
Well, nothing lasts, as Bacon came and said!
Here goes,—but keep your temper, or I 'll scream!

Fol-lol-the-rido-liddle-iddle-ol!
You see, sir, it 's your own fault more than mine;
It 's all your fault, you curious gentlefolk!
You 're prigs,—excuse me,—like to look so spry,
So clever, while you cling by half a claw
To the perch whereon you puff yourselves at roost,
Such piece of self-conceit as serves for perch
Because you chose it, so it must be safe.
Oh, otherwise you 're sharp enough! You spy
Who slips, who slides, who holds by help of wing,
Wanting real foothold,—who can't keep upright
On the other perch, your neighbour chose, not you:

There 's no outwitting you respecting him!
For instance, men love money—that, you know—
And what men do to gain it: well, suppose
A poor lad, say a help's son in your house,
Listening at keyholes, hears the company
Talk grand of dollars, V-notes, and so forth,
How hard they are to get, how good to hold,
How much they buy,—if, suddenly, in pops he—
" *I* 've got a V-note!"—what do you say to him?
What 's your first word which follows your last kick?
" Where did you steal it, rascal?" That 's because
He finds you, fain would fool you, off your perch,
Not on the special piece of nonsense, sir,
Elected your parade-ground: let him try
Lies to the end of the list,—" He picked it up,
His cousin died and left it him by will,
The President flung it to him, riding by,
An actress trucked it for a curl of his hair,
He dreamed of luck and found his shoe enriched,
He dug up clay, and out of clay made gold"—
How would you treat such possibilities?
Would not you, prompt, investigate the case
With cow-hide? " Lies, lies, lies," you 'd shout: and
    why?
Which of the stories might not prove mere truth?
This last, perhaps, that clay was turned to coin!

Let 's see, now, give him me to speak for him!
How many of your rare philosophers,
In plaguy books I 've had to dip into,
Believed gold could be made thus, saw it made
And made it? Oh, with such philosophers
You 're on your best behaviour! While the lad—
With him, in a trice, you settle likelihoods,
Nor doubt a moment how he got his prize:
In his case, you hear, judge and execute,
All in a breath: so would most men of sense.

But let the same lad hear you talk as grand
At the same keyhole, you and company,
Of signs and wonders, the invisible world;
How wisdom scouts our vulgar unbelief
More than our vulgarest incredulity;
How good men have desired to see a ghost,
What Johnson used to say, what Wesley did,
Mother Goose thought, and fiddle-diddle-dee:—
If he then break in with, " Sir, *I* saw a ghost!"
Ah, the ways change! He finds you perched and prim;
It 's a conceit of yours that ghosts may be:
There 's no talk now of cow-hide. " Tell it out!
Don't fear us! Take your time and recollect!
Sit down first: try a glass of wine, my boy!

And, David, (is not that your Christian name?)
Of all things, should this happen twice—it may—
Be sure, while fresh in mind, you let us know!"
Does the boy blunder, blurt out this, blab that,
Break down in the other, as beginners will?
All 's candour, all 's considerateness—" No haste!
Pause and collect yourself! We understand!
That 's the bad memory, or the natural shock,
Or the unexplained *phenomena!*"

         Egad,
The boy takes heart of grace; finds, never fear,
The readiest way to ope your own heart wide,
Show—what I call your peacock-perch, pet post
To strut, and spread the tail, and squawk upon!
" Just as you thought, much as you might expect!
There be more things in heaven and earth,
  Horatio," . .
And so on. Shall not David take the hint,
Grow bolder, stroke you down at quickened rate?
If he ruffle a feather, it 's " Gently, patiently!
Manifestations are so weak at first!.
Doubting, moreover, kills them, cuts all short,
Cures with a vengeance!"

       There, sir, that 's your style!
You and your boy—such pains bestowed on him,

Or any headpiece of the average worth,
To teach, say, Greek, would perfect him apace,
Make him a Person (" Porson?" thank you, sir!)
Much more, proficient in the art of lies.
You never leave the lesson! Fire alight,
Catch you permitting it to die! You 've friends;
There 's no withholding knowledge,—least from those
Apt to look elsewhere for their souls' supply:
Why should not you parade your lawful prize?
Who finds a picture, digs a medal up,
Hits on a first edition,—he henceforth
Gives it his name, grows notable: how much more,
Who ferrets out a " medium?" " David 's yours,
You highly-favoured man? Then, pity souls
Less privileged! Allow us share your luck!"
So, David holds the circle, rules the roast,
Narrates the vision, peeps in the glass ball,
Sets to the spirit-writing, hears the raps,
As the case may be.

     Now mark! To be precise—
Though I say, " lies " all these, at this first stage,
'Tis just for science' sake: I call such grubs
By the name of what they 'll turn to, dragonflies.
Strictly, it 's what good people style untruth;
But yet, so far, not quite the full-grown thing:

It 's fancying, fable-making, nonsense-work—
What never meant to be so very bad—
The knack of story-telling, brightening up
Each dull old bit of fact that drops its shine.
One does see somewhat when one shuts one's eyes,
If only spots and streaks; tables do tip
In the oddest way of themselves: and pens, good
    Lord,
Who knows if you drive them or they drive you?
'Tis but a foot in the water and out again;
Not that duck-under which decides your dive.
Note this, for it 's important: listen why.

I 'll prove, you push on David till he dives
And ends the shivering. Here 's your circle, now:
Two-thirds of them, with heads like you their host,
Turn up their eyes, and cry, as you expect,
" Lord, who 'd have thought it !" But there 's always
    one
Looks wise, compassionately smiles, submits
" Of your veracity no kind of doubt,
But—do you feel so certain of that boy's?
Really, I wonder! I confess myself
More chary of my faith!" That 's galling, sir!
What, he the investigator, he the sage,
When all 's done? Then, you just have shut your eyes,

Opened your mouth, and gulped down David whole,
You! Terrible were such catastrophe!
So, evidence is redoubled, doubled again,
And doubled besides; once more, "He heard, we heard,
You and they heard, your mother and your wife,
Your children and the stranger in your gates:
Did they or did they not?" So much for him,
The black sheep, guest without the wedding-garb,
And doubting Thomas! Now 's your turn to crow:
"He 's kind to think you such a fool: Sludge cheats?
Leave you alone to take precautions!"

         Straight
The rest join chorus. Thomas stands abashed,
Sips silent some such beverage as this,
Considers if it be harder, shutting eyes
And gulping David in good fellowship,
Than going elsewhere, getting, in exchange,
With no egg-nogg to lubricate the food,
Some just as tough a morsel. Over the way,
Holds Captain Sparks his court: is it better there?
Have not you hunting-stories, scalping-scenes,
And Mexican War exploits to swallow plump
If you 'd be free of the stove-side, rocking-chair,
And trio of affable daughters?

Doubt succumbs!
Victory! All your circle's yours again!
Out of the clubbing of submissive wits,
David's performance rounds, each chink gets patched,
Every protrusion of a point 's filed fine,
All 's fit to set a-rolling round the world,
And then return to David finally,
Lies seven-feet-thick about his first half-inch.
Here 's a choice birth of the supernatural,
Poor David 's pledged to! You 've employed no tool
That laws exclaim at, save the devil's own,
Yet screwed him into henceforth gulling you
To the top of your bent,—all out of one half-lie!

You hold, if there 's one half or a hundredth part
Of a lie, that 's his fault,—his be the penalty!
I dare say! You 'd prove firmer in his place?
You 'd find the courage,—that first flurry over,
That mild bit of romancing-work at end,—
To interpose with "It gets serious, this;
Must stop here. Sir, I saw no ghost at all.
Inform your friends I made . . well, fools of them,
And found you ready made. I 've lived in clover
These three weeks: take it out in kicks of me!"
I doubt it! Ask your conscience! Let me know,
Twelve months hence, with how few embellishments

You 've told almighty Boston of this passage
Of arms between us, your first taste of the foil
From Sludge who could not fence, sir! Sludge, your
    boy!
I lied, sir,—there! I got up from my gorge
On offal in the gutter, and preferred
Your canvass-backs: I took their carver's size,
Measured his modicum of intelligence,
Tickled him on the cockles of his heart
With a raven feather, and next week found myself
Sweet and clean, dining daintily, dizened smart,
Set on a stool buttressed by ladies' knees,
Every soft smiler calling me her pet,
Encouraging my story to uncoil
And creep out from its hole, inch after inch,
" How last night, I no sooner snug in bed,
Tucked up, just as they left me,—than came raps!
While a light whisked " . . " Shaped somewhat like
    a star?"
" Well, like some sort of stars, ma'am."—" So we
    thought!
And any voice? Not yet? Try hard, next time,
If you can't hear a voice; we think you may:
At least, the Pennsylvanian 'mediums' did."
Oh, next time comes the voice! " Just as we
    hoped!"

Are not the hopers proud now, pleased, profuse
Of the natural acknowledgment?

                                            Of course!
So, off we push, illy-oh-yo, trim the boat,
On we sweep with a cataract ahead,
We 're midway to the Horse-shoe : stop, who can,
The dance of bubbles gay about our prow!
Experiences become worth waiting for,
Spirits now speak up, tell their inmost mind,
And compliment the " medium " properly,
Concern themselves about his Sunday coat,
See rings on his hand with pleasure. Ask yourself
How you 'd receive a course of treats like these!
Why, take the quietest hack and stall him up,
Cram him with corn a month, then out with
    him
Among his mates on a bright April morn,
With the turf to tread ; see if you find or no
A caper in him, if he bucks or bolts!
Much more a youth whose fancies sprout as rank
As toadstool-clump from melon-bed. 'Tis soon,
" Sirrah, you spirit, come, go, fetch and carry,
Read, write, rap, rub-a-dub, and hang yourself!"
I 'm spared all further trouble ; all 's arranged ;
Your circle does my business ; I may rave

Like an epileptic dervish in the books,
Foam, fling myself flat, rend my clothes to shreds;
No matter: lovers, friends and countrymen
Will lay down spiritual laws, read wrong things
    right
By the rule of reverse. If Francis Verulam
Styles himself Bacon, spells the name beside
With a *y* and a *k*, says he drew breath in York,
Gave up the ghost in Wales when Cromwell reigned,
(As, sir, we somewhat fear he was apt to say,
Before I found the useful book that knows)
Why, what harm's done? The circle smiles apace,
"It was not Bacon, after all, do you see!
We understand; the trick's but natural:
Such spirits' individuality
Is hard to put in evidence: they incline
To gibe and jeer, these undeveloped sorts.
You see, their world's much like a jail broke loose,
While this of ours remains shut, bolted, barred,
With a single window to it. Sludge, our friend,
Serves as this window, whether thin or thick,
Or stained or stainless; he's the medium-pane
Through which, to see us and be seen, they peep:
They crowd each other, hustle for a chance,
Tread on their neighbour's kibes, play tricks enough!
Does Bacon, tired of waiting, swerve aside?

Up in his place jumps Barnum—'I 'm your man,
I 'll answer you for Bacon!' Try once more!"

Or else it 's—" What 's a 'medium'? He 's a means,
Good, bad, indifferent, still the only means
Spirits can speak by; he may misconceive,
Stutter and stammer,—he 's their Sludge and drudge,
Take him or leave him; they must hold their peace,
Or else, put up with having knowledge strained
To half-expression through his ignorance.
Suppose, the spirit Beethoven wants to shed
New music he 's brimfull of; why, he turns
The handle of this organ, grinds with Sludge,
And what he poured in at the mouth o' the mill
As a Thirty-third Sonata, (fancy now!)
Comes from the hopper as bran-new Sludge, nought
  else,
The Shakers' Hymn in G, with a natural F,
Or the 'Stars and Stripes' set to consecutive fourths."

Sir, where 's the scrape you did not help me through,
You that are wise? And for the fools, the folk
Who came to see,—the guests, (observe that word!)
Pray do you find guests criticize your wine,
Your furniture, your grammar, or your nose?
Then, why your "medium?" What 's the difference?

Prove your madeira red-ink and gamboge,—
Your Sludge, a cheat—then, somebody's a goose
For vaunting both as genuine. "Guests!" Don't
    fear!
They'll make a wry face, nor too much of that,
And leave you in your glory.

               "No, sometimes
They doubt and say as much!" Ay, doubt they do!
And what's the consequence? "Of course they
    doubt"—
(You triumph) "that explains the hitch at once!
Doubt posed our 'medium,' puddled his pure mind;
He gave them back their rubbish: pitch chaff in,
Could flour come out o' the honest mill?" So,
    prompt
Applaud the faithful: cases flock in point,
"How, when a mocker willed a 'medium' once
Should name a spirit James whose name was
    George,
'James' cried the 'medium,'—'twas the test of
    truth!"
In short, a hit proves much, a miss proves more.
Does this convince? The better: does it fail?
Time for the double-shotted broadside, then—
The grand means, last resource. Look black and big!

"You style us idiots, therefore—why stop short?
Accomplices in rascality: this we hear
In our own house, from our invited guest
Found brave enough to outrage a poor boy
Exposed by our good faith! Have you been
    heard?
Now, then, hear us; one man's not quite worth
    twelve.
You see a cheat? Here's some twelve see an ass:
Excuse me if I calculate: good day!"
Out slinks the sceptic, all the laughs explode,
Sludge waves his hat in triumph!

                         Or—he don't.
There's something in real truth (explain who can!)
One casts a wistful eye at, like the horse
Who mopes beneath stuffed hay-racks and won't
    munch
Because he spies a corn-bag: hang that truth,
It spoils all dainties proffered in its place!
I've felt at times when, cockered, cossetted
And coddled by the aforesaid company,
Bidden enjoy their bullying,—never fear,
But o'er their shoulders spit at the flying man,—
I've felt a child; only, a fractious child
That, dandled soft by nurse, aunt, grandmother,

Who keep him from the kennel, sun and wind,
Good fun and wholesome mud,—enjoined be sweet,
And comely and superior,—eyes askance
The ragged sons of the gutter at their game,
Fain would be down with them i' the thick of the
    filth,
Making dirt-pies, laughing free, speaking plain,
And calling granny the grey old cat she is.
I 've felt a spite, I say, at you, at them,
Huggings and humbug—gnashed my teeth to mark
A decent dog pass! It 's too bad, I say,
Ruining a soul so!

                But what 's "so," what 's fixed,
Where may one stop? Nowhere! The cheating 's
    nursed
Out of the lying, softly and surely spun
To just your length, sir! I 'd stop soon enough:
But you 're for progress. "All old, nothing new?
Only the usual talking through the mouth,
Or writing by the hand? I own, I thought
This would develop, grow demonstrable,
Make doubt absurd, give figures we might see,
Flowers we might touch. There 's no one doubts
    you, Sludge!
You dream the dreams, you see the spiritual sights,

The speeches come in your head, beyond dispute.
Still, for the sceptics' sake, to stop all mouths,
We want some outward manifestation!—well,
The Pennsylvanians gained such; why not Sludge?
He may improve with time!"

        Ay, that he may!
He sees his lot: there 's no avoiding fate.
'Tis a trifle at first. "Eh, David? Did you hear?
You jogged the table, your foot caused the squeak,
This time you 're . . . joking, are you not, my boy?"
"N-n-no!"—and I 'm done for, bought and sold
 henceforth.
The old good easy jog-trot way, the . . . eh?
The . . . not so very false, as falsehood goes,
The spinning out and drawing fine, you know,—
Really mere novel-writing of a sort,
Acting, or improvising, make-believe,
Surely not downright cheatery! Any how,
'Tis done with and my lot cast; Cheat 's my name:
The fatal dash of brandy in your tea
Has settled what you 'll have the souchong 's smack:
The caddy gives way to the dram-bottle.

Then, it 's so cruel easy! Oh, those tricks
That can't be tricks, those feats by sleight of hand,

Clearly no common conjuror's!—no, indeed!
A conjuror? Choose me any craft in the world
A man puts hand to; and with six months' pains,
I 'll play you twenty tricks miraculous
To people untaught the trade: have you seen glass
    blown,
Pipes pierced? Why, just this biscuit that I chip,
Did you ever watch a baker toss one flat
To the oven? Try and do it! Take my word,
Practise but half as much, while limbs are lithe,
To turn, shove, tilt a table, crack your joints,
Manage your feet, dispose your hands aright,
Work wires that twitch the curtains, play the glove
At end of your slipper,—then put out the lights
And ... there, there, all you want you 'll get, I
    hope!
I found it slip, easy as an old shoe.

Now, lights on table again! I 've done my part,
You take my place while I give thanks and rest.
"Well, Judge Humgruffin, what 's your verdict, sir?
You, hardest head in the United States,—
Did you detect a cheat here? Wait! Let 's see!
Just an experiment first, for candour's sake!
I 'll try and cheat you, Judge! The table tilts:
Is it I that move it? Write! I 'll press your hand:

Cry when I push, or guide your pencil, Judge!"
Sludge still triumphant! "That a rap, indeed?
That, the real writing? Very like a whale!
Then, if, sir, you—a most distinguished man,
And, were the Judge not here, I'd say, .. no matter!
Well, sir, if you fail, you can't take us in,—
There 's little fear that Sludge will!"

                                    Won't he, ma'am?
But what if our distinguished host, like Sludge,
Bade God bear witness that he played no trick,
While you believed that what produced the raps
Was just a certain child who died, you know,
And whose last breath you thought your lips had
    felt?
Eh? That 's a capital point, ma'am: Sludge begins
At your entreaty with your dearest dead,
The little voice set lisping once again,
The tiny hand made feel for yours once more,
The poor lost image brought back, plain as dreams,
Which image, if a word had chanced recall,
The customary cloud would cross your eyes,
Your heart return the old tick, pay its pang!
A right mood for investigation, this!
One 's at one 's ease with Saul and Jonathan,
Pompey and Cæsar: but one 's own lost child . . .

I wonder, when you heard the first clod drop
From the spadeful at the grave-side, felt you free
To investigate who twitched your funeral scarf
Or brushed your flounces? Then, it came of course,
You should be stunned and stupid; then, (how else?)
Your breath stopped with your blood, your brain
    struck work.
But now, such causes fail of such effects,
All 's changed,—the little voice begins afresh,
Yet you, calm, consequent, can test and try
And touch the truth. "Tests? Didn't the creature tell
Its nurse's name, and say it lived six years,
And rode a rocking-horse? Enough of tests!
Sludge never could learn that!"

                        He could not, eh?
You compliment him. "Could not?" Speak for
    yourself!
I 'd like to know the man I ever saw
Once,—never mind where, how, why, when,—once
    saw,
Of whom I do not keep some matter in mind
He 'd swear I "could not" know, sagacious soul!
What? Do you live in this world's blow of blacks,
Palaver, gossipry, a single hour
Nor find one smut has settled on your nose,

Of a smut's worth, no more, no less?—one fact
Out of the drift of facts, whereby you learn
What some one was, somewhere, somewhen, some-
    why?
You don't tell folk—" See what has stuck to me!
Judge Humgruffin, our most distinguished man,
Your uncle was a tailor, and your wife
Thought to have married Miggs, missed him, hit
    you!"—
Do you, sir, though you see him twice a-week?
" No," you reply, " what use retailing it?
Why should I?" But, you see, one day you *should*,
Because one day there's much use,—when this fact
Brings you the Judge upon both gouty knees
Before the supernatural; proves that Sludge
Knows, as you say, a thing he " could not " know:
Will not Sludge thenceforth keep an outstretched face,
The way the wind drives?

           " Could not!" Look you now,
I'll tell you a story! There's a whiskered chap,
A foreigner, that teaches music here
And gets his bread,—knowing no better way:
He says, the fellow who informed of him
And made him fly his country and fall West,
Was a hunchback cobbler, sat, stitched soles and sang,

In some outlandish place, the city Rome,
In a cellar by their Broadway, all day long;
Never asked questions, stopped to listen or look,
Nor lifted nose from lapstone; let the world
Roll round his three-legged stool, and news run in
The ears he hardly seemed to keep pricked up.
Well, that man went on Sundays, touched his pay,
And took his praise from government, you see;
For something like two dollars every week,
He 'd engage tell you some one little thing
Of some one man, which led to many more,
(Because one truth leads right to the world's end,)
And make you that man's master—when he dined
And on what dish, where walked to keep his health
And to what street. His trade was, throwing thus
His sense out, like an anteater's long tongue,
Soft, innocent, warm, moist, impassible,
And when 't was crusted o'er with creatures—slick,
Their juice enriched his palate. "Could not Sludge!"

I 'll go yet a step further, and maintain,
Once the imposture plunged its proper depth
In the rotten of your natures, all of you,—
(If one 's not mad nor drunk, and hardly then)
It 's impossible to cheat—that 's, be found out!
Go tell your brotherhood this first slip of mine,

All to-day's tale, how you detected Sludge,
Behaved unpleasantly, till he was fain confess,
And so has come to grief! You'll find, I think,
Why Sludge still snaps his fingers in your face.
There now, you've told them! What's their prompt
    reply?
" Sir, did that youth confess he had cheated me,
I 'd disbelieve him. He may cheat at times;
That's in the 'medium'-nature, thus they 're made,
Vain and vindictive, cowards, prone to scratch.
And so all cats are; still, a cat's the beast
You coax the strange electric sparks from out,
By rubbing back its fur; not so a dog,
Nor lion, nor lamb: 'tis the cat's nature, sir!
Why not the dog's? Ask God, who made them
    beasts!
D' ye think the sound, the nicely-balanced man
(Like me"—aside)—" like you yourself,"—(aloud)
" —He's stuff to make a 'medium?' Bless your soul,
'Tis these hysteric, hybrid half-and-halfs,
Equivocal, worthless vermin yield the fire!
We must take such as we find them, 'ware their tricks,
Wanting their service. Sir, Sludge took in you—
How, I can't say, not being there to watch:
He was tried, was tempted by your easiness,—
He did not take in me!"

       Thank you for Sludge!
I 'm to be grateful to such patrons, eh,
When what you hear 's my best word? 'Tis a chal-
    lenge;
" Snap at all strangers, you half-tamed prairie-dog,
So you cower duly at your keeper's nod!
Cat, show what claws were made for, muffling them
Only to me! Cheat others if you can,
Me, if you dare!" And, my wise sir, I dared—
Did cheat you first, made you cheat others next,
And had the help of your vaunted manliness
To bully the incredulous. You used me?
Have not I used you, taken full revenge,
Persuaded folk they knew not their own name,
And straight they 'd own the error! Who was the
    fool
When, to an awe-struck, wide-eyed, open-mouthed
Circle of sages, Sludge would introduce
Milton composing baby-rhymes, and Locke
Reasoning in gibberish, Homer writing Greek
In noughts and crosses, Asaph setting psalms
To crotchet and quaver? I 've made a spirit squeak
In sham voice for a minute, then outbroke
Bold in my own, defying the imbeciles—
Have copied some ghost's pothooks, half a page,
Then ended with my own scrawl undisguised.

" All right!   The ghost was merely using Sludge,
Suiting itself from his imperfect stock!"
Don't talk of gratitude to me!   For what?
For being treated as a showman's ape,
Encouraged to be wicked and make sport,
Fret or sulk, grin or whimper, any mood
So long as the ape be in it and no man—
Because a nut pays every mood alike.
Curse your superior, superintending sort,
Who, since you hate smoke, send up boys that climb
To cure your chimney, bid a "medium" lie
To sweep you truth down!   Curse your women too,
Your insolent wives and daughters, that fire up
Or faint away if a male hand squeeze theirs,
Yet, to encourage Sludge, may play with Sludge
As only a "medium," only the kind of thing
They must humour, fondle . . oh, to misconceive
Were too preposterous!   But I've paid them out!
They've had their wish—called for the naked truth,
And in she tripped, sat down and bade them stare:
They had to blush a little and forgive!
" The fact is, children talk so; in next world
All our conventions are reversed,—perhaps
Made light of: something like old prints, my dear!
The Judge has one, he brought from Italy,

A metropolis in the background,—o'er a bridge,
A team of trotting roadsters,—cheerful groups
Of wayside travellers, peasants at their work,
And, full in front, quite unconcerned, why not?
Three nymphs conversing with a cavalier,
And never a rag among them: 'fine,' folk cry—
And heavenly manners seem not much unlike!
Let Sludge go on; we'll fancy it's in print!"
If such as came for wool, sir, went home shorn,
Where is the wrong I did them? 'Twas their choice;
They tried the adventure, ran the risk, tossed up
And lost, as some one's sure to do in games;
They fancied I was made to lose,—smoked glass
Useful to spy the sun through, spare their eyes:
And had I proved a red-hot iron plate
They thought to pierce, and, for their pains, grew blind,
Whose were the fault but theirs? While, as things go,
Their loss amounts to gain, the more's the shame!
They've had their peep into the spirit-world,
And all this world may know it! They've fed fat
Their self-conceit which else had starved: what chance
Save this, of cackling o'er a golden egg
And compassing distinction from the flock,
Friends of a feather? Well, they paid for it,
And not prodigiously; the price o' the play,
Not counting certain pleasant interludes,

Was scarce a vulgar play's worth. When you buy
The actor's talent, do you dare propose
For his soul beside? Whereas, my soul you buy!
Sludge acts Macbeth, obliged to be Macbeth,
Or you will not hear his first word! Just go through
That slight formality, swear himself 's the Thane,
And thenceforth he may strut and fret his hour,
Spout, spawl, or spin his target, no one cares!
Why hadn't I leave to play tricks, Sludge as Sludge?
Enough of it all! I 've wiped out scores with you—
Vented your fustian, let myself be streaked
Like a tom-fool with your ochre and carmine,
Worn patchwork your respectable fingers sewed
To metamorphose somebody,—yes, I 've earned
My wages, swallowed down my bread of shame,
And shake the crumbs off—where but in your face?

As for religion—why, I served it, sir!
I'll stick to that! With my *phenomena*
I laid the atheist sprawling on his back,
And propped Saint Paul up, or, at least, Swedenborg!
In fact, it 's just the proper way to baulk
These troublesome fellows—liars, one and all,
Are not these sceptics? Well, to baffle them,
No use in being squeamish: lie yourself!
Erect your buttress just as wide o' the line,

Your side, as they 've built up the wall on theirs;
Where both meet, midway in a point, is truth,
High overhead: so, take your room, pile bricks,
Lie! Oh, there 's titillation in all shame!
What snow may lose in white, it gains in rose:
Miss Stokes turns—Rahab,—nor a bad exchange!
Glory be on her, for the good she wrought,
Breeding belief anew 'neath ribs of death,
Brow-beating now the unabashed before,
Ridding us of their whole life's gathered straws
By a live coal from the altar! Why, of old,
Great men spent years and years in writing books
To prove we 've souls, and hardly proved it then:
Miss Stokes with her live coal, for you and me!
Surely, to this good issue, all was fair—
Not only fondling Sludge, but, even suppose
He let escape some spice of knavery,—well,
In wisely being blind to it! Don't you praise
Nelson for setting spy-glass to blind eye
And saying . . what was it—that he could not see
The signal he was bothered? Ay, indeed!

I'll go beyond: there 's a real love of a lie,
Liars find ready-made for lies they make,
As hand for glove, or tongue for sugar-plum.
At best, 'tis never pure and full belief;

Those furthest in the quagmire,—don't suppose
They strayed there with no warning, got no chance
Of a filth-speck in their face, which they clenched
    teeth,
Bent brow against! Be sure they had their doubts,
And fears, and fairest challenges to try
The floor o' the seeming solid sand! But no!
Their faith was pledged, acquaintance too apprised,
All but the last step ventured, kerchiefs waved,
And Sludge called " pet :" 'twas easier marching on
To the promised land; join those who, Thursday
    next
Meant to meet Shakespeare; better follow Sludge—
Prudent, oh sure!—on the alert, how else?
But making for the mid-bog, all the same!
To hear your outcries, one would think I caught
Miss Stokes by the scuff o' the neck, and pitched her
    flat,
Foolish-face-foremost! Hear these simpletons,
That's all I beg, before my work's begun,
Before I 've touched them with my finger-tip!
Thus they await me (do but listen, now!
It 's reasoning, this is,—I can't imitate
The baby voice, though) " In so many tales
Must be some truth, truth though a pin-point big,
Yet, some: a single man 's deceived, perhaps—

Hardly, a thousand: to suppose one cheat
Can gull all these, were more miraculous far
Than aught we should confess a miracle "—
And so on. Then the Judge sums up—(it 's rare)—
Bids you respect the authorities that leap
To the judgment-seat at once,—why, don't you note
The limpid nature, the unblemished life,
The spotless honour, indisputable sense
Of the first upstart with his story? What—
Outrage a boy on whom you ne'er till now
Set eyes, because he finds raps trouble him?

Fools, these are: ay, and how of their opposites
Who never did, at bottom of their hearts,
Believe for a moment?—Men emasculate,
Blank of belief, who played, as eunuchs use,
With superstition safely,—cold of blood,
Who saw what made for them in the mystery,
Took their occasion, and supported Sludge
—As proselytes? No, thank you, far too shrewd!
—But promisers of fair play, encouragers
Of the claimant; who in candour needs must hoist
Sludge up on Mars' Hill, get speech out of Sludge
To carry off, criticize, and cant about!
Didn't Athens treat Saint Paul so?—at any rate,
It 's "a new thing," philosophy fumbles at.

Then there 's the other picker out of pearl
From dung heaps,—ay, your literary man,
Who draws on his kid gloves to deal with Sludge
Daintily and discreetly,—shakes a dust
Of the doctrine, flavours thence, he well knows how,
The narrative or the novel,—half-believes,
All for the book's sake, and the public's stare,
And the cash that 's God's sole solid in this world!
Look at him! Try to be too bold, too gross
For the master! Not you! He 's the man for muck;
Shovel it forth, full-splash, he 'll smooth your brown
Into artistic richness, never fear!
Find him the crude stuff; when you recognize
Your lie again, you 'll doff your hat to it,
Dressed out for company! "For company,"
I say, since there 's the relish of success:
Let all pay due respect, call the lie truth,
Save the soft silent smirking gentleman
Who ushered in the stranger: you must sigh
"How melancholy, he, the only one,
Fails to perceive the bearing of the truth
Himself gave birth to!"—There 's the triumph's smack!
That man would choose to see the whole world roll
I' the slime o' the slough, so he might touch the tip

Of his brush with what I call the best of browns—
Tint ghost-tales, spirit-stories, past the power
Of the outworn umber and bistre!

        Yet I think
There 's a more hateful form of foolery—
The social sage's, Solomon of saloons
And philosophic diner-out, the fribble
Who wants a doctrine for a chopping-block
To try the edge of his faculty upon,
Prove how much common sense he'll hack and hew
In the critical minute 'twixt the soup and fish!
These were my patrons: these, and the like of them
Who, rising in my soul now, sicken it,—
These I have injured! Gratitude to these?
The gratitude, forsooth, of a prostitute
To the greenhorn and the bully—friends of hers,
From the wag that wants the queer jokes for his
  club,
To the snuff-box-decorator, honest man,
Who just was at his wits' end where to find
So genial a Pasiphae! All and each
Pay, compliment, protect from the police,
And how she hates them for their pains, like me!
So much for my remorse at thanklessness
Toward a deserving public!

                              But, for God?
Ay, that's a question! Well, sir, since you press—
(How you do teaze the whole thing out of me!
I don't mean you, you know, when I say " them:"
Hate you, indeed!   But that Miss Stokes, that
      Judge!
Enough, enough—with sugar: thank you, sir!)
Now for it, then!   Will you believe me, though?
You've heard what I confess; I don't unsay
A single word: I cheated when I could,
Rapped with my toe-joints, set sham hands at work,
Wrote down names weak in sympathetic ink,
Rubbed odic lights with ends of phosphor-match,
And all the rest; believe that: believe this,
By the same token, though it seem to set
The crooked straight again, unsay the said,
Stick up what I've thrown down; I can't help that:
It's truth! I somehow vomit truth to-day.
This trade of mine—I don't know, can't be sure
But there was something in it, tricks and all!
Really, I want to light up my own mind.
They were tricks,—true, but what I mean to add
Is also true.   First,—don't it strike you, sir?
Go back to the beginning,—the first fact
We're taught is, there's a world beside this world,
With spirits, not mankind, for tenantry;

That much within that world once sojourned here,
That all upon this world will travel there,
And therefore that we, bodily here below,
Must have exactly such an interest
In learning what may be the ways o' the world
Above us, as the disembodied folk
Have (by all analogic likelihood)
In watching how things go in the old world
With us, their sons, successors, and what not.
Oh, yes, with added powers probably,
Fit for the novel state,—old loves grown pure,
Old interests understood aright,—they watch!
Eyes to see, ears to hear, and hands to help,
Proportionate to advancement: they 're ahead,
That 's all—do what we do, but noblier done—
Use plate, whereas we eat our meals off delf,
(To use a figure.)

    Concede that, and I ask
Next, what may be the mode of intercourse
Between us men here, and those once-men there?
First comes the Bible's speech; then, history
With the supernatural element,—you know—
All that we sucked in with our mothers' milk,
Grew up with, got inside of us at last,
Till it 's found bone of bone and flesh of flesh.

See now, we start with the miraculous,
And know it used to be, at all events:
What's the first step we take, and can't but take,
In arguing from the known to the obscure?
Why this: "What was before, may be to-day.
Since Samuel's ghost appeared to Saul,—of course
My brother's spirit may appear to me."
Go tell your teacher that! What's his reply?
What brings a shade of doubt for the first time
O'er his brow late so luminous with faith?
"Such things have been," says he, "and there's no doubt
Such things may be: but I advise mistrust
Of eyes, ears, stomach, and, more than all, your brain,
Unless it be of your great-grandmother,
Whenever they propose a ghost to you!"
The end is, there's a composition struck;
'Tis settled, we've some way of intercourse
Just as in Saul's time; only, different:
How, when and where, precisely,—find it out!
I want to know, then, what's so natural
As that a person born into this world
And seized on by such teaching, should begin
With firm expectancy and a frank look-out
For his own allotment, his especial share

In the secret,—his particular ghost, in fine?
I mean, a person born to look that way,
Since natures differ: take the painter-sort,
One man lives fifty years in ignorance
Whether grass be green or red,—" No kind of eye
For colour," say you; while another picks
And puts away even pebbles, when a child,
Because of bluish spots and pinky veins—
" Give him forthwith a paint-box!" Just the same
Was I born . . . " medium," you won't let me say,—
Well, seer of the supernatural
Everywhen, everyhow and everywhere,—
Will that do?

      I and all such boys of course
Started with the same stock of bible-truth;
Only,—what in the rest you style their sense,
Instinct, blind reasoning but imperative,
This, betimes, taught them the old world had one law
And ours another: "New world, new laws," cried they:
" None but old laws, seen everywhere at work,"
Cried I, and by their help explained my life
The Jews' way, still a working way to me.
Ghosts made the noises, fairies waved the lights,
Or Santaclaus slid down on New Year's Eve
And stuffed with cakes the stocking at my bed,

Changed the worn shoes, rubbed clean the fingered
    slate
Of the sum that came to grief the day before.

This could not last long: soon enough I found
Who had worked wonders thus, and to what end:
But did I find all easy, like my mates?
Henceforth no supernatural any more?
Not a whit: what projects the billiard-balls?
"A cue," you answer: "Yes, a cue," said I;
"But what hand, off the cushion, moved the cue?
What unseen agency, outside the world,
Prompted its puppets to do this and that,
Put cakes and shoes and slates into their mind,
These mothers and aunts, nay even schoolmasters?"
Thus high I sprang, and there have settled since.
Just so I reason, in sober earnest still,
About the greater godsends, what you call
The serious gains and losses of my life.
What do I know or care about your world
Which either is or seems to be? This snap
Of my fingers, sir! My care is for myself;
Myself am whole and sole reality
Inside a raree-show and a market-mob
Gathered about it: that's the use of things.
'Tis easy saying they serve vast purposes,

Advantage their grand selves: be it true or
    false,
Each thing may have two uses. What 's a star?
A world, or a world's sun: doesn't it serve
As taper also, time-piece, weather-glass,
And almanac? Are stars not set for signs
When we should shear our sheep, sow corn, prune
    trees?
The Bible says so.

              Well, I add one use
To all the acknowledged uses, and declare
If I spy Charles's Wain at twelve to-night,
It warns me, " Go, nor lose another day,
And have your hair cut, Sludge!" You laugh: and
    why?
Were such a sign too hard for God to give?
No: but Sludge seems too little for such grace:
Thank you, sir! So you think, so does not Sludge!
When you and good men gape at Providence,
Go into history and bid us mark
Not merely powder-plots prevented, crowns
Kept on kings' heads by miracle enough,
But private mercies—oh, you 've told me, sir,
Of such interpositions! How yourself
Once, missing on a memorable day

Your handkerchief—just setting out, you know,—
You must return to fetch it, lost the train,
And saved your precious self from what befell
The thirty-three whom Providence forgot.
You tell, and ask me what I think of this?
Well, sir, I think then, since you needs must know,
What matter had you and Boston city to boot
Sailed skyward, like burnt onion-peelings? Much
To you, no doubt: for me—undoubtedly
The cutting of my hair concerns me more,
Because, however sad the truth may seem,
Sludge is of all-importance to himself.
You set apart that day in every year
For special thanksgiving, were a heathen else:
Well, I who cannot boast the like escape,
Suppose I said " I don't thank Providence
For my part, owing it no gratitude ?"
" Nay, but you owe as much "—you 'd tutor me,
" You, every man alive, for blessings gained
In every hour of the day, could you but know!
I saw my crowning mercy: all have such,
Could they but see!" Well, sir, why don't they
    see ?
" Because they won't look,—or perhaps, they can't."
Then, sir, suppose I can, and will, and do
Look, microscopically as is right,

Into each hour with its infinitude
Of influences at work to profit Sludge?
For that 's the case: I 've sharpened up my sight
To spy a providence in the fire's going out,
The kettle's boiling, the dime's sticking fast
Despite the hole i' the pocket. Call such facts
Fancies, too petty a work for Providence,
And those same thanks which you exact from me,
Prove too prodigious payment: thanks for what,
If nothing guards and guides us little men?
No, no, sir! You must put away your pride,
Resolve to let Sludge into partnership!
I live by signs and omens: looked at the roof
Where the pigeons settle—" If the further bird,
The white, takes wing first, I 'll confess when thrashed;
Not, if the blue does "—so I said to myself
Last week, lest you should take me by surprise:
Off flapped the white,—and I 'm confessing, sir!
Perhaps 'tis Providence's whim and way
With only me, in the world: how can you tell?
" Because unlikely!" Was it likelier, now,
That this our one out of all worlds beside,
The what-d'you-call-'em millions, should be just
Precisely chosen to make Adam for,
And the rest o' the tale? Yet the tale 's true, you
    know:

Such undeserving clod was gracëd so once;
Why not graced likewise undeserving Sludge?
Are we merit-mongers, flaunt we filthy rags?
All you can bring against my privilege
Is, that another way was taken with you,—
Which I don't question. It's pure grace, my luck.
I'm broken to the way of nods and winks,
And need no formal summoning. You've a help;
Holloa his name or whistle, clap your hands,
Stamp with your foot or pull the bell: all's one,
He understands you want him, here he comes.
Just so, I come at the knocking: you, sir, wait
The tongue of the bell, nor stir before you catch
Reason's clear tingle, nature's clapper brisk,
Or that traditional peal was wont to cheer
Your mother's face turned heavenward: short of
    these
There's no authentic intimation, eh?
Well, when you hear, you'll answer them, start up
And stride into the presence, top of toe,
And there find Sludge beforehand, Sludge that sprung
At noise o' the knuckle on the partition-wall!
I think myself the more religious man.
Religion's all or nothing; it's no mere smile
Of contentment, sigh of aspiration, sir—
No quality of the finelier-tempered clay

Like its whiteness or its lightness; rather, stuff
Of the very stuff, life of life, self of self.
I tell you, men won't notice; when they do,
They'll understand. I notice nothing else,
I'm eyes, ears, mouth of me, one gaze and gape,
Nothing eludes me, everything's a hint,
Handle and help. It's all absurd, and yet
There's something in it all, I know: how much?
No answer! What does that prove? Man's still man,
Still meant for a poor blundering piece of work
When all's done; but, if somewhat's done, like this,
Or not done, is the case the same? Suppose
I blunder in my guess at the true sense
Of the knuckle-summons, nine times out of ten,—
What if the tenth guess happen to be right?
If the tenth shovel-load of powdered quartz
Yield me the nugget? I gather, crush, sift all,
Pass o'er the failure, pounce on the success.
To give you a notion, now—(let who wins, laugh!)
When first I see a man, what do I first?
Why, count the letters which make up his name,
And as their number chances, even or odd,
Arrive at my conclusion, trim my course:
Hiram H. Horsefall is your honoured name,
And have n't I found a patron, sir, in you?
"Shall I cheat this stranger?" I take apple-pips,

Stick one in either *canthus* of my eye,
And if the left drops first—(your left, sir, stuck)
I 'm warned, I let the trick alone this time.
You, sir, who smile, superior to such trash,
You judge of character by other rules:
Don't your rules sometimes fail you? Pray, what
    rule
Have you judged Sludge by hitherto?

                              Oh, be sure,
You, everybody blunders, just as I,
In simpler things than these by far! For see:
I knew two farmers,—one, a wiseacre,
Who studied seasons, rummaged almanacs,
Quoted the dew-point, registered the frost,
And then declared, for outcome of his pains,
Next summer must be dampish: 't was a drought.
His neighbour prophesied such drought would fall,
Saved hay and corn, made cent. per cent. thereby,
And proved a sage indeed: how came his lore?
Because one brindled heifer, late in March,
Stiffened her tail of evenings, and somehow
He got into his head that drought was meant!
I don't expect all men can do as much:
Such kissing goes by favour. You must take
A certain turn of mind for this,—a twist

I' the flesh, as well. Be lazily alive,
Open-mouthed, like my friend the anteater,
Letting all nature's loosely-guarded motes
Settle and, slick, be swallowed! Think yourself
The one i' the world, the one for whom the world
Was made, expect it tickling at your mouth!
Then will the swarm of busy buzzing flies,
Clouds of coincidence, break egg-shell, thrive,
Breed, multiply, and bring you food enough.

I can't pretend to mind your smiling, sir!
Oh, what you mean is this! Such intimate way,
Close converse, frank exchange of offices,
Strict sympathy of the immeasurably great
With the infinitely small, betokened here
By a course of signs and omens, raps and sparks,—
How does it suit the dread traditional text
Of the "Great and Terrible Name?" Shall the
    Heaven of Heavens
Stoop to such child's-play?

                Please sir, go with me
A moment, and I 'll try to answer you.
The "*Magnum et terribile*" (is that right?)
Well, folk began with this in the early day;
And all the acts they recognized in proof

Were thunders, lightnings, earthquakes, whirlwinds,
    dealt
Indisputably on men whose death they caused.
There, and there only, folk saw Providence
At work,—and seeing it, 'twas right enough
All heads should tremble, hands wring hands amain,
And knees knock hard together at the breath
Of the Name's first letter; why, the Jews, I 'm told,
Won't write it down, no, to this very hour,
Nor speak aloud: you know best if 't be so.
Each ague-fit of fear at end, they crept
(Because somehow people once born must live)
Out of the sound, sight, swing and sway of the Name,
Into a corner, the dark rest of the world,
And safe space where as yet no fear had reached;
'T was there they looked about them, breathed again,
And felt indeed at home, as we might say.
The current of common things, the daily life,
This had their due contempt; no Name pursued
Man from the mountain-top where fires abide,
To his particular mouse-hole at its foot
Where he ate, drank, digested, lived in short:
Such was man's vulgar business, far too small
To be worth thunder: "small," folk kept on, "small,"
With much complacency in those great days!
A mote of sand, you know, a blade of grass—

What was so despicable as mere grass,
Except perhaps the life of the worm or fly
Which fed there? These were "small" and men
    were great.
Well, sir, the old way 's altered somewhat since,
And the world wears another aspect now:
Somebody turns our spyglass round, or else
Puts a new lens in it: grass, worm, fly grow big:
We find great things are made of little things,
And little things go lessening till at last
Comes God behind them. Talk of mountains now?
We talk of mould that heaps the mountain, mites
That throng the mould, and God that makes the
    mites.
The Name comes close behind a stomach-cyst,
The simplest of creations, just a sac
That 's mouth, heart, legs and belly at once, yet
    lives
And feels, and could do neither, we conclude,
If simplified still further one degree:
The small becomes the dreadful and immense!
Lightning, forsooth? No word more upon that!
A tin-foil bottle, a strip of greasy silk,
With a bit of wire and knob of brass, and there 's
Your dollar's-worth of lightning! But the cyst—
The life of the least of the little things?

                        No, no!
Preachers and teachers try another tack,
Come near the truth this time: they put aside
Thunder and lightning: "That's mistake," they cry,
" Thunderbolts fall for neither fright nor sport,
But do appreciable good, like tides,
Changes of the wind, and other natural facts—
' Good' meaning good to man, his body or soul.
Mediate, immediate, all things minister
To man,—that 's settled: be our future text
' We are His children!'" So, they now harangue
About the intention, the contrivance, all
That keeps up an incessant play of love,—
See the Bridgewater book.

                        Amen to it!
Well, sir, I put this question: I 'm a child?
I lose no time, but take you at your word:
How shall I act a child's part properly?
Your sainted mother, sir,—used you to live
With such a thought as this a-worrying you?
" She has it in her power to throttle me,
Or stab or poison: she may turn me out,
Or lock me in,—nor stop at this, to-day,
But cut me off to-morrow from the estate
I look for "— (long may you enjoy it, sir!)

"In brief, she may unchild the child I am."
You never had such crotchets? Nor have I!
Who, frank confessing childship from the first,
Cannot both fear and take my ease at once,
So, don't fear,—know what might be, well enough,
But know too, child-like, that it will not be,
At least in my case, mine, the son and heir
Of the kingdom, as yourself proclaim my style.
But do you fancy I stop short at this?
Wonder if suit and service, sons and heirs
Needs must expect, I dare pretend to find?
If, looking for signs proper to such an one,
I straight perceive them irresistible?
Concede that homage is a son's plain right,
And, never mind the nods and raps and winks,
'Tis the pure obvious supernatural
Steps forward, does its duty: why, of course!
I have presentiments; my dreams come true:
I fancy a friend stands whistling all in white
Blithe as a boblink, and he's dead I learn.
I take dislike to a dog my favourite long,
And sell him; he goes mad next week and snaps.
I guess that stranger will turn up to-day
I have not seen these three years; there's his knock.
I wager "sixty peaches on that tree!"—
That I pick up a dollar in my walk,

That your wife's brother's cousin's name was George—
And win on all points. Oh, you wince at this?
You 'd fain distinguish between gift and gift,
Washington's oracle and Sludge's itch
O' the elbow when at whist he ought to trump?
With Sludge it 's too absurd? *Fine, draw the line*
Somewhere, but, sir, your somewhere is not mine!

Bless us, I 'm turning poet! It 's time to end.
How you have drawn me out, sir! All I ask
Is—am I heir or not heir? If I 'm he,
Then, sir, remember, that same personage
(To judge by what we read in the newspaper)
Requires, beside one nobleman in gold
To carry up and down his coronet,
Another servant, probably a duke,
To hold egg-nogg in readiness : why want
Attendance, sir, when helps in his father's house
Abound, I 'd like to know?

       Enough of talk!
My fault is that I tell too plain a truth.
Why, which of those who say they disbelieve,
Your clever people, but has dreamed his dream,
Caught his coincidence, stumbled on his fact
He can't explain, (he 'll tell you smilingly)

Which he 's too much of a philosopher
To count as supernatural, indeed,
So calls a puzzle and problem, proud of it:
Bidding you still be on your guard, you know,
Because one fact don't make a system stand,
Nor prove this an occasional escape
Of spirit beneath the matter: that 's the way!
Just so wild Indians picked up, piece by piece,
The fact in California, the fine gold
That underlay the gravel—hoarded these,
But never made a system stand, nor dug!
So wise men hold out in each hollowed palm
A handful of experience, sparkling fact
They can't explain; and since their rest of life
Is all explainable, what proof in this?
Whereas I take the fact, the grain of gold,
And fling away the dirty rest of life,
And add this grain to the grain each fool has found
Of the million other such philosophers,—
Till I see gold, all gold and only gold,
Truth questionless though unexplainable,
And the miraculous proved the commonplace!
The other fools believed in mud, no doubt—
Failed to know gold they saw: was that so strange?
Are all men born to play Bach's fiddle-fugues,
" Time " with the foil in carte, jump their own height,

Cut the mutton with the broadsword, skate a five,
Make the red hazard with the cue, clip nails
While swimming, in five minutes row a mile,
Pull themselves three feet up with the left arm,
Do sums of fifty figures in their head,
And so on, by the scores of instances?
The Sludge with luck, who sees the spiritual facts,
His fellows strive and fail to see, may rank
With these, and share the advantage!

         Ay, but share
The drawback! Think it over by yourself;
I have not heart, sir, and the fire's gone grey.
Defect somewhere compensates for success,
Everyone knows that! Oh, we're equals, sir!
The big-legged fellow has a little arm
And a less brain, though big legs win the race:
Do you suppose I 'scape the common lot?
Say, I was born with flesh so sensitive,
Soul so alert, that, practice helping both,
I guess what's going on outside the veil,
Just as a prisoned crane feels pairing-time
In the islands where his kind are, so must fall
To capering by himself some shiny night,
As if your back-yard were a plot of spice—
Thus am I 'ware of the spirit-world: while you,

Blind as a beetle that way,—for amends,
Why, you can double fist and floor me, sir!
Ride that hot, hardmouthed, horrid horse of yours,
Laugh while it lightens, play with the great dog,
Speak your mind though it vex some friend to hear,
Never brag, never bluster, never blush,—
In short, you've pluck, when I'm a coward—there!
I know it, I can't help it,—folly or no,
I'm paralyzed, my hand's no more a hand,
Nor my head, a head, in danger: you can smile
And change the pipe in your cheek. Your gift's not
    mine.
Would you swap for mine? No! but you'd add my
    gift
To yours: I dare say! I too sigh at times,
Wish I were stouter, could tell truth nor flinch,
Kept cool when threatened, did not mind so much
Being dressed gaily, making strangers stare,
Eating nice things; when I'd amuse myself,
I shut my eyes and fancy in my brain
I'm—now the President, now, Jenny Lind,
Now, Emerson, now, the Benicia Boy—
With all the civilized world a-wondering
And worshipping! I know it's folly and worse:
I feel such tricks sap, honeycomb the soul,
But I can't cure myself,—despond, despair,

And then, hey, presto, there's a turn of the wheel,
Under comes uppermost, fate makes full amends;
Sludge knows and sees and hears a hundred things
You all are blind to,—I've my taste of truth,
Likewise my touch of falsehood,—vice no doubt,
But you've your vices also: I'm content.

What, sir? You won't shake hands? "Because I
    cheat!
You've found me out in cheating!" That's enough
To make an apostle swear! Why, when I cheat,
Mean to cheat, do cheat, and am caught in the act,
Are you, or rather, am I sure of the fact?
(There's verse again, but I'm inspired somehow.)
Well then, I'm not sure! I may be, perhaps,
Free as a babe from cheating: how it began,
My gift,—no matter; what 'tis got to be
In the end now, that's the question: answer that!
Had I seen, perhaps, what hand was holding mine,
Leading me whither, I had died of fright,
So, I was made believe I led myself.
If I should lay a six-inch plank from roof
To roof, you would not cross the street, one step,
Even at your mother's summons: but, being shrewd,
If I paste paper on each side of the plank
And swear 'tis solid pavement, why, you'll cross

Humming a tune the while, in ignorance
Beacon Street stretches a hundred feet below:
I walked thus, took the paper-cheat for stone.
Some impulse made me set a thing on the move
Which, started once, ran really by itself;
Beer flows thus, suck the siphon; toss the kite,
It takes the wind and floats of its own force.
Don't let truth's lump rot stagnant for the lack
Of a timely helpful lie to leaven it!
Put a chalk-egg beneath the clucking hen,
She 'll lay a real one, laudably deceived,
Daily for weeks to come. I 've told my lie,
And seen truth follow, marvels none of mine;
All was not cheating, sir, I 'm positive!
I don't know if I move your hand sometimes
When the spontaneous writing spreads so far,
If my knee lifts the table all that height,
Why the inkstand don't fall off the desk a-tilt.
Why the accordion plays a prettier waltz
Than I can pick out on the piano-forte,
Why I speak so much more than I first intend,
Describe so many things I never saw.
I tell you, sir, in one sense, I believe
Nothing at all,—that everybody can,
Will, and does cheat: but in another sense
I 'm ready to believe my very self—

That every cheat 's inspired, and every lie
Quick with a germ of truth.

      You ask perhaps
Why I should condescend to trick at all
If I know a way without it? This is why!
There 's a strange secret sweet self-sacrifice
In any desecration of one's soul
To a worthy end,—isn't it Herodotus
(I wish I could read Latin!) who describes
The single gift of the land's virginity,
Demanded in those old Egyptian rites,
(I 've but a hazy notion—help me, sir!)
For one purpose in the world, one day in a life,
One hour in the day—thereafter, purity,
And a veil thrown o'er the past for evermore!
Well now, they understood a many things
Down by Nile city, or wherever it was!
I 've always vowed, after the minute's lie,
And the good end's gain,—truth should be mine
  henceforth.
This goes to the root of the matter, sir,—this plain
Plump fact: accept it and unlock with it
The wards of many a puzzle!

      Or, finally,
Why should I set so fine a gloss on things?

What need I care? I cheat in self-defence,
And there 's my answer to a world of cheats!
Cheat? To be sure, sir! What 's the world worth
    else?
Who takes it as he finds, and thanks his stars?
Don't it want trimming, turning, furbishing up
And polishing over? Your so-styled great men,
Do they accept one truth as truth is found,
Or try their skill at tinkering? What 's your
    world?
Here are you born, who are, I 'll say at once,
One of the luckiest whether in head and heart,
Body and soul, or all that helps the same.
Well, now, look back: what faculty of yours
Came to its full, had ample justice done
By growing when rain fell, biding its time,
Solidifying growth when earth was dead,
Spiring up, broadening wide, in seasons due?
Never! You shot up and frost nipped you off,
Settled to sleep when sunshine bade you sprout;
One faculty thwarted its fellow: at the end,
All you boast is, "I had proved a topping tree
In other climes"—yet this was the right clime
Had you foreknown the seasons. Young, you 've
    force
Wasted like well-streams: old,—oh, then indeed,

Behold a labyrinth of hydraulic pipes
Through which you 'd play off wondrous water-
    work;
Only, no water left to feed their play!
Young,—you 've a hope, an aim, a love; it 's tossed
And crossed and lost: you struggle on, some spark
Shut in your heart against the puffs around,
Through cold and pain; these in due time subside,
Now then for age's triumph, the hoarded light
You mean to loose on the altered face of things,—
Up with it on the tripod! It 's extinct.
Spend your life's remnant asking, which was best,
Light smothered up that never peeped forth once,
Or the cold cresset with full leave to shine?
Well, accept this too,—seek the fruit of it
Not in enjoyment, proved a dream on earth,
But knowledge, useful for a second chance,
Another life, — you 've lost this world — you 've
    gained
Its knowledge for the next. — What knowledge,
    sir,
Except that you know nothing? Nay, you doubt
Whether 'twere better have made you man or brute,
If aught be true, if good and evil clash.
No foul, no fair, no inside, no outside,
There 's your world!

Give it me! I slap it brisk
With harlequin's pasteboard sceptre: what's it now?
Changed like a rock-flat, rough with rusty weed,
At first wash-over of the returning wave!
All the dry, dead, impracticable stuff
Starts into life and light again; this world
Pervaded by the influx from the next.
I cheat, and what's the happy consequence?
You find full justice straightway dealt you out,
Each want supplied, each ignorance set at ease,
Each folly fooled. No life-long labour now
As the price of worse than nothing! No mere film
Holding you chained in iron, as it seems,
Against the outstretch of your very arms
And legs in the sunshine moralists forbid!
What would you have? Just speak and, there, you
    see!
You're supplemented, made a whole at last,
Bacon advises, Shakespeare writes you songs,
And Mary Queen of Scots embraces you.
Thus it goes on, not quite like life perhaps,
But so near, that the very difference piques,
Shows that e'en better than this best will be—
This passing entertainment in a hut
Whose bare walls take your taste since, one stage
    more,

And you arrive at the palace: all half real,
And you, to suit it, less than real beside,
In a dream, lethargic kind of death in life,
That helps the interchange of natures, flesh
Transfused by souls, and such souls! Oh, 'tis choice!
And if at whiles the bubble, blown too thin,
Seem nigh on bursting,—if you nearly see
The real world through the false,—what *do* you
 see?
Is the old so ruined? You find you 're in a flock
Of the youthful, earnest, passionate—genius, beauty,
Rank and wealth also, if you care for these,
And all depose their natural rights, hail you,
(That 's me, sir) as their mate and yoke-fellow,
Participate in Sludgehood—nay, grow mine,
I veritably possess them—banish doubt,
And reticence and modesty alike!
Why, here 's the Golden Age, old Paradise
Or new Eutopia! Here is life indeed,
And the world well won now, yours for the first time!

And all this might be, may be, and with good help
Of a little lying shall be: so, Sludge lies!
Why, he 's at worst your poet who sings how Greeks
That never were, in Troy which never was,
Did this or the other impossible great thing!

He 's Lowell—it 's a world, you smile and say,
Of his own invention—wondrous Longfellow,
Surprising Hawthorne ! Sludge does more than they,
And acts the books they write : the more 's his
    praise !

But why do I mount to poets ? Take plain prose—
Dealers in common sense, set these at work,
What can they do without their helpful lies ?
Each states the law and fact and face of the thing
Just as he 'd have them, finds what he thinks fit,
Is blind to what missuits him, just records
What makes his case out, quite ignores the rest.
It 's a History of the World, the Lizard Age,
The Early Indians, the Old Country War,
Jerome Napoleon, whatsoever you please,
All as the author wants it. Such a scribe
You pay and praise for putting life in stones,
Fire into fog, making the past your world.
There 's plenty of " How did you contrive to grasp
The thread which led you through this labyrinth ?
How build such solid fabric out of air ?
How on so slight foundation found this tale,
Biography, narrative ?" or, in other words,
" How many lies did it require to make
The portly truth you here present us with ?"

"Oh," quoth the penman, purring at your praise,
" 'Tis fancy all; no particle of fact:
I was poor and threadbare when I wrote that book
'Bliss in the Golden City.' I, at Thebes?
We writers paint out of our heads, you see!"
" Ah, the more wonderful the gift in you,
The more creativeness and godlike craft!"
But I, do I present you with my piece,
It's "What, Sludge? When my sainted mother
    spoke
The verses Lady Jane Grey last composed
About the rosy bower in the seventh heaven
Where she and Queen Elizabeth keep house,—
You made the raps? 'T was your invention that?
Cur, slave and devil!"—eight fingers and two thumbs
Stuck in my throat!

            Well, if the marks seem gone,
'Tis because stiffish cock-tail, taken in time,
Is better for a bruise than arnica.

There, sir! I bear no malice: 'tis n't in me.
I know I acted wrongly: still, I 've tried
What I could say in my excuse,—to show
The devil 's not all devil . . . I don't pretend,
An angel, much less such a gentleman

As you, sir! And I've lost you, lost myself,
Lost all, l-l-l- . . . .

    No—are you in earnest, sir?
O, yours, sir, is an angel's part! I know
What prejudice must be, what the common course
Men take to soothe their ruffled self-conceit:
Only you rise superior to it all!
No, sir, it don't hurt much; it's speaking long
That makes me choke a little: the marks will go!
What? Twenty V-notes more, and outfit too,
And not a word to Greeley? One—one kiss
Of the hand that saves me! You'll not let me
  speak, .
I well know, and I've lost the right, too true!
But I must say, sir, if She hears (she does)
Your sainted . . . Well, sir,—be it so! That's, I
  think,
My bed-room candle. Good night! Bl-l-less you, sir!

R-r-r, you brute-beast and blackguard! Cowardly
  scamp!
I only wish I dared burn down the house
And spoil your sniggering! Oh, what, you're the
  man?

You 're satisfied at last? You 've found out Sludge?
We 'll see that presently : my turn, sir, next!
I too can tell my story: brute,—do you hear?—
You throttled your sainted mother, that old hag,
In just such a fit of passion : no, it was . . .
To get this house of hers, and many a note
Like these . . . I 'll pocket them, however . . . five,
Ten, fifteen . . . ay, you gave her throat the twist,
Or else you poisoned her! Confound the cuss!
Where was my head? I ought to have prophesied
He 'll die in a year and join her : that 's the way.

I don't know where my head is : what had I done?
How did it all go? I said he poisoned her,
And hoped he 'd have grace given him to repent,
Whereon he picked this quarrel, bullied me
And called me cheat: I thrashed him,—who could
    help?
He howled for mercy, prayed me on his knees
To cut and run and save him from disgrace :
I do so, and once off, he slanders me.
An end of him! Begin elsewhere anew!
Boston 's a hole, the herring-pond is wide,
V-notes are something, liberty still more.
Beside, is he the only fool in the world?

APPARENT FAILURE.

APPARENT FAILURE.

"We shall soon lose a celebrated building."
Paris Newspaper.

1.

No, for I 'll save it! Seven years since,
  I passed through Paris, stopped a day
To see the baptism of your Prince;
  Saw, made my bow, and went my way:
Walking the heat and headache off,
  I took the Seine-side, you surmise,
Thought of the Congress, Gortschakoff,
  Cavour's appeal and Buol's replies,
So sauntered till—what met my eyes?

2.

Only the Doric little Morgue!
   The dead-house where you show your drowned:
Petrarch's Vaucluse makes proud the Sorgue,
   Your Morgue has made the Seine renowned.
One pays one's debt in such a case;
   I plucked up heart and entered,—stalked,
Keeping a tolerable face
   Compared with some whose cheeks were chalked:
Let them! No Briton 's to be baulked!

3.

First came the silent gazers; next,
   A screen of glass, we 're thankful for;
Last, the sight's self, the sermon's text,
   The three men who did most abhor
Their life in Paris yesterday,
   So killed themselves: and now, enthroned
Each on his copper couch, they lay
   Fronting me, waiting to be owned.
I thought, and think, their sin 's atoned.

4.

Poor men, God made, and all for that!
    The reverence struck me; o'er each head
Religiously was hung its hat,
    Each coat dripped by the owner's bed,
Sacred from touch: each had his berth,
    His bounds, his proper place of rest,
Who last night tenanted on earth
    Some arch, where twelve such slept abreast,—
Unless the plain asphalte seemed best.

5.

How did it happen, my poor boy?
    You wanted to be Buonaparte
And have the Tuileries for toy,
    And could not, so it broke your heart?
You, old one by his side, I judge,
    Were, red as blood, a socialist,
A leveller! Does the Empire grudge
    You've gained what no Republic missed?
Be quiet, and unclench your fist!

6.

And this—why, he was red in vain,
  Or black,—poor fellow that is blue!
What fancy was it, turned your brain?
  Oh, women were the prize for you!
Money gets women, cards and dice
  Get money, and ill-luck gets just
The copper couch and one clear nice
  Cool squirt of water o'er your bust,
The right thing to extinguish lust!

7.

It 's wiser being good than bad;
  It 's safer being meek than fierce:
It 's fitter being sane than mad.
  My own hope is, a sun will pierce
The thickest cloud earth ever stretched;
  That, after Last, returns the First,
Though a wide compass round be fetched;
  That what began best, can't end worst,
Nor what God blessed once, prove accurst.

EPILOGUE.

EPILOGUE.

FIRST SPEAKER, as *David*.

1.

On the first of the Feast of Feasts,
    The Dedication Day,
When the Levites joined the Priests
    At the Altar in robed array,
Gave signal to sound and say,—

2.

When the thousands, rear and van,
    Swarming with one accord,
Became as a single man,
    (Look, gesture, thought and word)
In praising and thanking the Lord,—

3.

When the singers lift up their voice,
    And the trumpets made endeavour,
Sounding, " In God rejoice !"
    Saying, " In Him rejoice
Whose mercy endureth for ever !"—

4.

Then the Temple filled with a cloud,
    Even the House of the Lord ;
Porch bent and pillar bowed :
    For the presence of the Lord,
In the glory of His cloud,
    Had filled the House of the Lord.

SECOND SPEAKER, *as Renan.*

Gone now ! All gone across the dark so far,
    Sharpening fast, shuddering ever, shutting still,
Dwindling into the distance, dies that star
    Which came, stood, opened once ! We gazed our fill
With upturned faces on as real a Face
    That, stooping from grave music and mild fire,
Took in our homage, made a visible place
    Through many a depth of glory, gyre on gyre,

For the dim human tribute. Was this true?
　Could man indeed avail, mere praise of his,
To help by rapture God's own rapture too,
　Thrill with a heart's red tinge that pure pale bliss?
Why did it end? Who failed to beat the breast,
　And shriek, and throw the arms protesting wide,
When a first shadow showed the star addressed
　Itself to motion, and on either side
The rims contracted as the rays retired;
　The music, like a fountain's sickening pulse,
Subsided on itself; awhile transpired
　Some vestige of a Face no pangs convulse,
No prayers retard; then even this was gone,
　Lost in the night at last. We, lone and left
Silent through centuries, ever and anon
　Venture to probe again the vault bereft
Of all now save the lesser lights, a mist
　Of multitudinous points, yet suns, men say—
And this leaps ruby, this lurks amethyst,
　But where may hide what came and loved our clay?
How shall the sage detect in yon expanse
　The star which chose to stoop and stay for us?
Unroll the records! Hailed ye such advance
　Indeed, and did your hope evanish thus?
Watchers of twilight, is the worst averred?
　We shall not look up, know ourselves are seen,

Speak, and be sure that we again are heard,
    Acting or suffering, have the disk's serene
Reflect our life, absorb an earthly flame,
    Nor doubt that, were mankind inert and numb,
Its core had never crimsoned all the same,
    Nor, missing ours, its music fallen dumb?
Oh, dread succession to a dizzy post,
    Sad sway of sceptre whose mere touch appals,
Ghastly dethronement, cursed by those the most
    On whose repugnant brow the crown next falls!

THIRD SPEAKER.

1.

Witless alike of will and way divine,
How Heaven's high with earth's low should intertwine!
Friends, I have seen through your eyes: now use mine.

2.

Take the least man of all mankind, as I;
Look at his head and heart, find how and why
He differs from his fellows utterly:

3.

Then, like me, watch when nature by degrees
Grows alive round him, as in Arctic seas
(They said of old) the instinctive water flees

4.

Toward some elected point of central rock,
As though, for its sake only, roamed the flock
Of waves about the waste : awhile they mock

5.

With radiance caught for the occasion,—hues
Of blackest hell now, now such reds and blues
As only heaven could fitly interfuse,—

6.

The mimic monarch of the whirlpool, king
O' the current for a minute : then they wring
Up by the roots and oversweep the thing,

7.

And hasten off, to play again elsewhere
The same part, choose another peak as bare,
They find and flatter, feast and finish there.

8.

When you see what I tell you,—nature dance
About each man of us, retire, advance,
As though the pageant's end were to enhance

9.

His worth, and—once the life, his product, gained—
Roll away elsewhere, keep the strife sustained,
And show thus real, a thing the North but feigned,—

10.

When you acknowledge that one world could do
All the diverse work, old yet ever new,
Divide us, each from other, me from you,—

11.

Why, where 's the need of Temple, when the walls
O' the world are that? What use of swells and falls
From Levites' choir, Priests' cries, and trumpet-calls?

12.

That one Face, far from vanish, rather grows,
Or decomposes but to recompose,
Become my universe that feels and knows!

www.ingramcontent.com/pod-product-compliance
Lightning Source LLC
Chambersburg PA
CBHW021405230426
43666CB00006B/646